D0951995

HOW TO USE COOPERATIVE LEARNING IN THE MATHEMATICS CLASS

SECOND EDITION

Alice F. Artzt
and
Claire M. Newman

Queens College
of the
City University of New York

NATIONAL COUNCIL OF TEACHERS OF MATHEMATICS
Reston, Virginia

Library of Congress Cataloging-in-Publication Data:

Artzt, Alice F.
    How to use cooperative learning in the mathematics class / Alice
F. Artzt and Claire M. Newman. — 2nd ed.
        p.   cm.
    Includes bibliographical references.
    ISBN 0-87353-437-9 (pbk .)
    1. Group work in education. 2. Mathematics—Study and teaching.
I. Newman, Claire M.   II. Title.
QA 16.A78 1997
510′ .71—dc21   97-26980
                                                                      CIP

Printed in the United States of America

CONTENTS

PREFACE

Much has happened since the first edition of this book was published. Cooperative learning has gone from an innovative teaching strategy, used by only a few teachers who had the courage and creativity to try it, to a strategy important to many who teach mathematics. The cooperative learning approach has been supported not only by national mathematics organizations. Research on how people learn has also suggested that learning is a social process and that cooperative learning activities are essential if students are to be able to construct their own knowledge. In the past several years, many teachers, teacher educators, and researchers have studied and tried a variety of cooperative learning approaches. Much has been learned. This new edition includes many new ideas and techniques that we and other people have used. The updated bibliography lists many new articles and books that have been published since the first edition.

INTRODUCTION

Cooperation is essential to the progress of human civilization. It is as relevant to the interactions of nations as it is to the operations of business organizations. It is as important to the success of sports teams as it is to the advancement of science. It is as valuable to the functioning of families as it is to the relationships of individuals. Moreover, our population's diversity requires the individual to accept and work with others who are different from themselves. Regardless of race, ability, or handicap, students should learn that it is in their best interest to cooperate for the common good.

In recent years, the mathematics reform movement has suggested that teachers make greater use of cooperative learning approaches in their mathematics classes (e.g., NCSM 1989; NCTM 1989, 1991; NRC 1989). The reasons for this suggestion, however, go far beyond the recognition that cooperation in and of itself is an important skill for students to acquire. The suggestion is based on results of new learning theories that indicate the importance of small-group settings in which students communicate with their peers in constructing new ideas (e.g., Noddings 1990; Vygotsky 1978; Webb 1989). It is also based on voluminous reports from both researchers and teachers who have documented positive experiences and effects of small-group approaches in mathematics (e.g., Artzt 1979, 1994; Bassarear and Davidson 1992; Qin, Johnson, and Johnson 1995; Smith, Williams, and Wynn 1995; Sutton 1992).

Cooperation in the Classroom

For people to cooperate, they should first believe that cooperation has personal value for them. They should then develop certain skills and understandings. School systems that are built largely on recognizing individual accomplishments usually do not help students see the value in cooperation or help them develop cooperative skills. Unless schools create specific activities and reward structures that support cooperation, students may be deprived of enriching learning opportunities. Ultimately, they may lack the skills they need to function in an adult society. The classroom is a good setting for cooperative learning. Students afforded the opportunity to work in small groups can begin to practice the cooperative skills necessary for group members to solve problems together. Furthermore, each group member can learn the content of the curriculum through his or her interactions with the other members.

Cooperation in the Mathematics Classroom

Among many other national organizations, support for cooperative learning comes from the National Council of Teachers of Mathematics. The Council's

1

Curriculum and Evaluation Standards for School Mathematics (1989) recommends that teachers provide opportunities for students to work together in small groups to solve problems. In this way students can talk about the problem under consideration, discuss solution strategies, relate the problem to others that have been solved before, resolve difficulties, and think about the entire problem-solving process. According to the *Standards*, "Small groups provide a forum in which students ask questions, discuss ideas, make mistakes, learn to listen to others' ideas, offer constructive criticism, and summarize their discoveries in writing" (p. 79). Group assignments allow learners to work together, helping one another integrate new knowledge with prior knowledge and construct their own meanings as they explore, discuss, explain, relate, and question new ideas.

Just what is cooperative learning, and how can we make it work in the mathematics class?

WHAT IS COOPERATIVE LEARNING?

Cooperative learning involves a small group of learners who work together as a team to solve a problem, complete a task, or accomplish a common goal. There are many different cooperative learning techniques; all of them, however, have certain elements in common. These elements are the ingredients necessary to insure that when students *do* work in groups, they work cooperatively. First, group members must perceive that they are part of a team and that they all have a common goal. Second, group members must realize that the problem they will solve is a group problem and that all members will share the group's success or failure. Third, to accomplish the group's goal, all students must talk with one

another—to discuss all problems. Finally, it must be clear to all that each member's individual work has a direct effect on the group's success. Teamwork is important.

It is *not* sufficient to direct a group of students to separate into small groups and work on a problem or a set of problems. It is *not* cooperative learning if students sit together in groups and work on problems individually. It is *not* cooperative learning if students sit together in groups and let one person do all the work. True cooperative learning requires the guidance of a teacher who can help students understand group dynamics, develop the cooperative learning skills they need, and learn mathematics by working together in groups. Furthermore, true cooperative learning requires a teacher's ability to form productive groups, design appropriate tasks, enforce a motivating reward structure, and assess the group process continually. By encouraging student-to-student interaction, cooperative learning takes advantage of peer presence for increased and enriched learning opportunities.

Research Results: Positive Outcomes

Positive outcomes of cooperative learning strategies have been well documented by studies conducted at all grade levels and in all subjects (Johnson and Johnson 1989; Qin, Johnson, and Johnson 1995; Sharan 1980; Sharan 1990; Slavin 1990). Some of these research projects have compared cooperative learning methods with whole-class methods. Others have examined the individual and group processes in cooperating teams. Most of the accepted cooperative learning strategies promote forming groups that are heterogeneous in many ways. That is, groups may consist of students of different abilities and ethnic backgrounds, and they may include handicapped students. Such heterogeneity appears to lead to positive academic and social outcomes (Johnson and Johnson 1989).

Strong evidence indicates that cooperative learning benefits students across many dimensions (Johnson and Johnson 1990, 1995; Johnson, Johnson, and Maruyama 1983; Slavin 1990). Cooperative learning capitalizes on the powerful influence of peer relationships. By promoting interaction in the group, cooperative learning teaches students to support and accept students who are different. When placed in a working group, students of different abilities, cultural backgrounds, and physical makeups have common ground for discourse. Working together and getting to know one another have proved highly successful in removing artificial barriers and prejudices created by ignorance and unfamiliarity.

It is well documented that positive attitudes toward mathematics play a role in a student's ability to learn mathematics (Ma and Kishor 1997). Research indicates that cooperative learning experiences in the mathematics classroom foster improved attitudes toward the subject matter and the instruction (Johnson and Johnson 1991). The individual builds confidence in his or her own ability to do mathematics and thereby relieves math anxiety. Collaboration that takes place in a cooperative group gives each student the opportunity to help and receive help in a private, nonthreatening way. The small-group setting provides a comfortable social environment.

When students of different abilities are grouped together, opportunities abound for giving and receiving explanations. Contrary to what one might expect, the high-ability student benefits as much from group interaction as the low- or average-ability student (Johnson and Johnson 1992c). The verbal communication of mathematics is a means for students to become actively involved in learning mathematics. To give a mathematical explanation to one's peers, a student must understand the material in far more depth than that required merely to produce an answer on a worksheet. Research suggests, however, that for maximum communication, the ability range in the groups should not be too wide (Webb 1991). It is important also that all group members believe in the value of the group process. This is especially important for the high-ability group members who seem to have the most potential for setting the environment for communication within the group (Artzt and Armour-Thomas 1997).

The importance of peer relationships in a classroom should not be taken lightly. Children of all ages are influenced by their peers. If the classroom is structured cooperatively, peer influence can be used to positive ends. Students want their peers to do well. After all, an individual's success depends on the success of the group. Students want their peers to be prepared with the work and to be attentive and productive in class. Peer pressure for academic achievement is one of the most important factors contributing to the many positive outcomes of cooperative learning. Students are motivated to do well, to be prepared with their work, and to be attentive during class time, for these are the behaviors that lead to peer approval and group success.

Cooperative learning strategies have been credited with promoting critical thinking, higher-level thinking, and improved problem-solving ability (Johnson and Johnson 1989, 1992a; Qin, Johnson, and Johnson 1995). Current research examining behaviors that occur during group problem-solving sessions seems to indicate that groups engage in behaviors similar to those exhibited by mathematicians when they solve problems; that is, groups monitor their own thoughts, the thoughts of their teammates, and the status of the problem-solving process. They thereby often avoid the thoughtless wild-goose chases so characteristic of novice problem solvers working alone (Artzt and Armour-Thomas 1992; Curcio and Artzt 1992).

As research has documented, however, the positive outcomes from cooperative learning approaches will most likely occur only when they are carefully structured to ensure positive interdependence, individual accountability, face-to-face verbal communication, and positive social interaction in each group (Johnson and Johnson 1991; Slavin 1989). By attending to the following five areas, teachers can maximize their chances for making cooperative learning work: group formation, task designs, reward structures, ongoing assessment, and classroom management. The next section will discuss these five essential areas, addressing the questions most often asked about how to create an effective cooperative learning environment.

MAKING IT WORK
IN THE MATHEMATICS CLASS

Group Formation

Groups can be formed in many different ways, each serving a different purpose. Teachers can create groups that are heterogeneous in ability or personal characteristics, they can use a random assignment method, or they can allow students to select their own groups. The groups should stay together long enough to develop cohesiveness. Furthermore, to ensure success, groups must be small enough to need everyone but large enough to permit a diversity of ideas and skills.

How Should Students Be Assigned to Groups?

Creating heterogeneous groups can have many advantages. For example, if the groups are heterogeneous in ability, then students can readily give help to, or receive help from, one another. Students who are members of ethnically diverse groups can learn more about one another. The most effective way of ensuring heterogeneity is for the teacher to set up the groups. Teachers know their own students best and can see to it that they place readers with nonreaders, task-oriented students with non-task-oriented students, high-ability students with medium- and low-ability students, minority students with nonminority students, non-English-speaking students with those who speak English, handicapped students with nonhandicapped students, and females with males. It works well when teachers ask students to indicate with which peers they would like to work and consider their wishes when groups are being formed. It is important that students be happy in their groups if they are to work effectively.

Students can be assigned to groups randomly. This method is particularly useful at the beginning of the school year when the teacher has little information about the class. Students can count off, or names can be placed on slips of paper and drawn from a bag. Older students can learn about random numbers when the teacher uses a table of random numbers to assign them to their groups.

Students can select their own groups. In this method, students usually select friends or peers very much like themselves—same sex, same ethnic background, same ability, or the like. This tends to produce homogeneous groups and very often leaves out certain students entirely. Although this can be a good method for creating groups in which most students feel comfortable, it can result in too much off-task behavior caused by students' familiarity with one another.

How Frequently Should Group Membership Be Changed?

One of the criteria for group success is the durability of the group. Developing group cohesiveness takes time. When students know that their group will be together for some time, they realize that they must improve their interpersonal skills so that they can function effectively. Over time, they come to recognize their responsibilities to the group. Peer pressure often facilitates this recognition.

Cooperative learning groups may stay together for a unit of work, a semester, or a year. Students, however, must be satisfied with fellow group members if they are to feel comfortable enough to express their ideas freely and be productive in their groups. It is, therefore, necessary for the teacher to keep well informed about each group member's attitudes and behaviors. This can be done by overseeing students' interactions as they work together. Since looks can often be deceiving, it is important to give students the opportunity in private journal entries to express their feelings about their group members and their satisfaction with their groups. Through these techniques, the teacher can help the students learn to understand one another better and improve their cooperation. When necessary, the teacher may find that rearranging the groups will benefit everyone.

Certainly something can be said for giving students the opportunity to use their experiences in a new group setting. A new group means new relationships, new ideas and opinions, and new friends. Once a teacher has had some experience incorporating group work into the class, she or he will know when it is desirable or appropriate to form new groups.

How Many Students Should Be in Each Group?

The size of a group affects its ability to be productive. Experience has shown that groups of three to four students work well (Davidson 1990a). Although it is often advantageous for students to work in pairs, a cooperative learning group of just two members has a distinct disadvantage. Interaction is limited, and the group is vulnerable to either member's absence.

Conversely, if a group has too many students, it becomes very difficult for the group to function effectively. The most vocal students tend to take over, and the quiet ones recede into the background. In a large group, it is difficult for all members to air their ideas. Furthermore, it is difficult for a large group to get organized, coordinate its members' work, and reach agreement.

How Is Team Spirit Created?

Once the groups are formed, the students can agree on a name for their group. This gives the students the chance to talk about their interests and commonalities. They can get to know one another better in an informal setting. They can design a team logo. Students enjoy the chance to be creative and usually rise to the occasion. After receiving the teams' names and logos, the teacher can create and display a chart with the information for all to see. This team-building activity gives students a feeling of camaraderie and team spirit that is helpful for successful cooperative interactions among group members.

Team building can be accomplished through any activities that are enjoyable, are within each group member's capabilities, and help students get acquainted. For example, a beginning activity can have students introduce themselves to the other members of the team. The teacher might ask them to describe such things as their favorite activities outside school, their favorite subjects in school, or their past experiences in mathematics. The students might then introduce their fellow group members to the whole class by describing the information that was shared with them. This technique not only helps students get to know one another better but also gives them practice listening to one another, since they know they will have to repeat the information to the class. Mary Male (1990) suggests a getting-acquainted activity in which students complete a computer-made crossword puzzle whose clues concern each person in the group. Other team-building activities can be found in Anderson (1988), Dees (1990), Graves and Graves (1988), and Johnson and Johnson (1985).

Task Designs

For cooperative learning to succeed, students must believe that they depend on one another and that they are individually accountable for the work. To reinforce these perceptions, it is helpful to structure the tasks so that each student in the group must contribute to the group's work. That is, design the problem so that group members depend on one another to complete the task. Group members will then understand that they are responsible for one another. Each person is expected to learn the material and help others do the same.

How Can Each Student Be Motivated to Participate?

Although it is true that in cooperative learning groups, responsibility for each person's learning is shared by other group members, individual students must be held accountable for their own learning and for their contributions to the group. Each member of the group is responsible for understanding the work.

One way of ensuring that each student participates in the group assignment is having each student prepare the work before the group's meeting. This work can take the form of homework or an in-class assignment. The essential point is that each student be required to do individual work on the task before the group meets to compare and discuss approaches and strategies. This will not only ensure that they have done the work but also give them some basis for contributing when they meet with their group.

Another means of ensuring that each student participates is dividing the task so that each student has the responsibility for doing one part of the work. The students then realize that they must do the assigned work to enable their group to complete its task. The group holds its members individually accountable for such assignments.

Randomly selecting members from each group to be spokespersons—to explain their group's solutions or final products to the class—is another way of ensuring individual accountability. Individual group members realize that they must be involved actively in the work and discussions. If they do not understand something, they must question their group members for clarification because any member may be selected to present the group's work. Individuals cannot sit back and defer to others. They are expected to learn and participate in the group's work.

For cooperative learning to succeed, the students in a group must perceive themselves as dependent on one another. To achieve the group's goal or complete the group's task, each member expects each of the others to contribute. It is not enough for one person to be generous or altruistic while others accept what is given. Cooperation is based on reciprocity. Maintaining effective working relationships among group members requires each student to appreciate the value of reciprocation. Each student must be prepared to give as well as to receive.

The methods described above to ensure individual accountability also work to ensure mutual support among students. They encourage students to be concerned not only about themselves but also about the other members of the group. Students engage in peer teaching because they acknowledge that each group member must understand the material. Each student recognizes that group members expect him or her to complete the assigned work and to make a contribution to the group. Students help one another. One student explains a difficult concept to another in his or her own words. Group members share resources and act as resources for one another. Students divide up their responsibilities in the group. They may take on different roles, such as facilitator, reader, reporter, recorder, encourager, praiser, explainer, elaborator, organizer, checker, accuracy coach, summarizer, calculator user, and keyboarder. Students encourage one another to participate. Even those who are usually silent are made to feel that the group relies on them to participate. It's "all for one and one for all" because that is what makes group success possible.

Incentives and Reward Structures

What Makes Cooperative Learning Attractive to Students?

There are many reasons for students to want to work and learn together in groups. Most important is the intrinsic motivation for cooperative learning. The social aspects of group work are enjoyable. Students form new friendships and learn to appreciate differences—differences in ability, differences in personal characteristics, and differences of opinion. Students find that learning together is fun and that being part of a group is exciting. The student who helps others experiences gratification in giving. The students who know that they can depend on other group members for help and support are relieved of the anxiety often experienced by those who don't understand the work. A real sense of satisfaction comes from learning, achieving, and solving problems together. Cooperative learning can be truly rewarding.

Well-designed reward structures can give added incentives for positive small-group learning behaviors among students. One way of doing this is for the teacher and students to evaluate each group's product after it has been submitted. Each group's score should be recorded on a chart accessible to all students. There are many ways group products can be evaluated, depending on the nature of the assignments. Scoring may involve counting the number of correct solutions, using a rubric to evaluate a solution strategy qualitatively with a number or letter grade, or ranking the work from each group. Groups may compete with one another or strive to meet certain preestablished criteria.

To further ensure individual accountability and mutual dependence among students, a group might receive full credit for its results only if a randomly selected student in the group can adequately explain the group's work, results, and conclusions. Such a reward structure encourages students to check with one another to be sure that each person in the group understands the concepts, agrees with the solutions or conclusions, and can speak for the group. Students are likely to ask one another for help or clarification and ask and answer questions.

As an additional incentive, teachers may wish to give students group rewards. These rewards can take many different forms. For young children stickers may do well. Students can brainstorm lists of rewards. A handmade certificate can be awarded to the Group Champ of the Week. Applause should follow the presentation of the award, and the group's name should be placed on the bulletin board for all to see. Older children are always interested in improving their grades. Rewarding students in this way, however, must be done with care. Since successful group work is an indication of active participation of all group members, it is reasonable to count cooperation as a percent of the final grade. Many teachers also factor in participation. Therefore, members of successful groups may all be given extra "cooperation" points.

Ongoing Assessment

The *Assessment Standards for School Mathematics* states that assessment strategies must be "aligned with, and integral to, instruction" (NCTM 1995, p. 1). The complexity of the cooperative learning strategy necessitates using multiple and varied methods of assessment. Teachers and students need to assess the groups continually so as to ensure cooperative learning's continued effectiveness. When a group is functioning poorly, the teacher and students should be aware of it and come to understand the nature of the problem and why it is happening. The teacher must observe the groups carefully; the students must be called on to assess their own and their group members' behaviors. The teacher should provide feedback so that students know how well they are doing. The teacher may ask the groups to monitor their own performance by answering questions about the group's behavior and functioning. Is each person participating? Are students helping one another? Are they handling conflicts well? What do they understand about the mathematics they have learned together? The teacher, along with the students, can then agree on appropriate measures to improve the situation. Assessment techniques that focus on verbal communications about mathematics, interpersonal and group skills, and mathematical understanding will help the teacher and students improve the cooperative learning setting.

How Are Students' Verbal Communications about Mathematics Assessed?

Learning in a group necessitates verbal communication about mathematics. To work together, people must talk with one another about the task at hand and about what they are doing and thinking. The quality of the verbal interaction is an important factor in the group's success. When assessing students as they work in their small groups, teachers and students should look for certain types of verbal interaction.

In a successful cooperative learning group, students communicate, explain, and justify ideas and, when necessary, engage in intellectual conflict. A group should be involved in verbal conflict—conflict over ideas. Group members should be critical of ideas but not of people. Students should feel comfortable about disagreeing openly because such controversy strengthens their own understanding and helps the group reach consensus.

When a group is functioning well, each member has something to say and the opportunity to say it. Each person listens carefully to what other group members are saying and tries to understand ideas with which he or she disagrees. Each member tries to bring out all ideas before accepting a strategy or an answer. Before deciding on a problem-solving strategy, students should brainstorm ideas and discuss the approaches that seem appropriate.

Students in a successful cooperative learning group eagerly check with one another to be sure that each person understands the material, agrees with the results or conclusions, and can represent the group as a spokesperson. They ask one another for help or clarification. They also offer to explain or clarify mathematics concepts and methods. Concepts are summarized aloud. Students explain to one another how new knowledge relates to the material that has come before. They ask questions, and they answer questions.

When assessing these types of verbal interactions, teachers can use a checklist of students' names and such categories as Listens Carefully to Others,

Challenges Other Ideas, and Explains Ideas to Others. Students can address these categories in their journals. They can describe instances in which they helped someone understand something and instances in which someone helped them understand something. By engaging in this open type of assessment, students learn the types of verbal interaction that are valued for successful cooperative learning.

How Are Students' Collaborative Skills Assessed?

The quality of certain interpersonal and group skills determines how well people work together. Students need to develop cooperation skills if they are to function well in groups, be they cooperative learning groups, families, business organizations, or communities. For cooperative learning to succeed, students must master those collaborative skills that enable them to work effectively with others, no matter what their abilities or personal characteristics. It is helpful when both teachers and students observe and assess the collaborative skills of all group members.

Communication is necessary for people to cooperate. People must be able to communicate their ideas and feelings in a way that others will understand. These messages can be verbal or nonverbal, but they must be expressed in such a manner that the person receiving the message clearly understands what is meant. To be certain that the receiver understands what is being communicated, he or she can restate what has been said or ask one or more questions designed to clarify the message.

Trust is another important ingredient of cooperation. When there is trust, people are willing to be open in communicating their ideas and feelings. A person expresses trust when he or she is willing to share ideas with others in the group. People trust other members of the group when they perceive that others accept their ideas and are warm toward them. They believe that others recognize the value of their contributions. Trust is nourished when people support one another and convey the belief that each person can be a productive member of the group. The person who praises others for their contributions, encourages everyone to participate, shares materials with others, and offers to help others is a person who can be trusted.

For members of a group to cooperate and to complete their task, they must share the responsibility for taking on a leadership role. It is important for someone to help the group get started and stay on task; someone must coordinate the group's efforts; someone must give direction to the group's work; and someone must encourage participation. A person who can accomplish any of these goals in a warm, friendly, nonthreatening manner displays the skills of a leader.

It is not unusual for differences and disagreements to arise even though the group is working cooperatively. Group members need the skills to manage such controversies. They must ask questions. They need to clarify differences. Each person must be patient and exert self-control. Once all ideas have been discussed, group members must be willing to compromise—to integrate different perspectives into a single group solution that is acceptable to all. Such skills of conflict management are essential to the functioning of any group.

When assessing these types of collaborative skills, teachers can use a checklist of students' names and such categories as Accepts Ideas of Others, Praises Others for Their Ideas, Helps Keep the Group on Task, Helps Resolve Conflict within the Group. Students can address these categories in their journals. They can describe instances when they praised a group member for his or her idea or when they helped keep the group on task. This open type of assessment teaches students the communication skills that are valued for successful cooperative learning.

How Can Mathematical Understanding Be Assessed in Groups?

Discourse in a group can reveal much about students' understanding of mathematics. The teacher can monitor and record students' problem-solving behaviors as they work in groups. For example, the teacher can indicate on a chart which students are making comments that indicate higher-level problem-solving behaviors: *understanding* the problem by explaining it in their own words, *analyzing* the problem by relating it to something learned before or breaking it into smaller components, and *planning* an approach for the group to take in the solution of the problem. Other problem-solving behaviors such as *exploring, implementing,* and *verifying* can also be indicated through what the students write or say as they monitor their group members' problem-solving efforts. Finally, if one person is randomly selected to explain the group's solution, that person's mathematical understanding can be assessed.

When work is submitted by a group, it is sometimes difficult to assess the understanding of individual group members. It is, therefore, advisable to include a component that allows for this individual assessment. For example, after completing a group project, students can submit individual reports that address the following questions: What were your contributions to the group project? What did the other members of your group contribute to the project? What did you learn from having done the project? The students' responses can give the teacher a clearer picture of the mathematical understandings of the individual group members. In addition, if the teacher is assigning a group grade for the project, this technique allows for the teacher to be able to adjust the group grade accordingly for each student. For example, if a maximum score for a group product is 20 and the maximum score for the individual report is 10, group members can achieve the maximum score of 30 points only if they have indicated a thorough understanding of the group work.

Managing Cooperative Learning

How Is the Class Organized?

For students to work in small groups, it is important that the room be organized in such a way that members of a group are close enough to one another to work together comfortably and talk with one another quietly. Conversely, the groups must be separated so that they do not interfere with one another.

Before asking students to work in groups, give them the explanations of the assignment, the time allotted for the activity, the academic expectations for the group, the expected collaborative behaviors, the procedures to follow, and the desired outcomes for group success.

How Do You Get Students' Attention?

While students are working in their groups, it is sometimes necessary to get their attention. One technique that does not entail raising one's voice is for the teacher to raise a hand and require that each student who sees the hand raised do the same and stop talking. Then each student who sees another student's hand raised must do the same. The chain reaction stops when everyone has his or her hand raised and the class is quiet and attentive to the teacher. Other effective techniques are turning the lights on and off or ringing a bell.

Needless to say, as teachers become comfortable with the cooperative learning approach, they will decide for themselves how best to facilitate the cooperative learning process. Teachers who want to try cooperative learning for the first time can be overwhelmed and alarmed by all they must consider. To begin, however, it is not necessary that everything be structured to the smallest detail. An informal start is often a good way to begin. One possible way to get started follows.

Getting Started: An Example

Introducing cooperative learning in the mathematics lesson can be done in several ways. The teacher has many questions to consider before getting started. At what point in the lesson should the students form groups? For what purpose should the groups be used? For review of the homework? For review of the classwork? For experimentation and discovery leading to the development of the lesson? For test review? How should the groups be formed? Should the students be allowed to choose their own groups? Should the students be assigned to groups randomly, or should they be assigned using specific criteria?

Once the groups are formed, the teacher has other questions to consider. How should the tasks and reward systems be structured to encourage maximum participation of students within their groups? Should the groups compete with one another? Should there be rewards or incentives? What should be the criteria for receiving an award?

None of these questions has one correct answer. There are many options for the teacher to consider. One way of getting into the cooperative learning mode is to try it out with a homework assignment: Advise students that they will be participating in group problem solving. Suggest that they form their own groups of three to five members. (The teacher's role in facilitating the grouping will be discussed later.) To begin, have the members of each group compare their solutions to the previous night's assignment. Ask students to discuss their work with other members of the group and to come to an agreement on the best solutions. Then ask each group to submit one set of solutions. Next, lead a discussion based on the difficulties the students have encountered. Keep a record of each group's performance, and make the standings available to the class. To add enjoyment to the new class structure and help group members bond with one another, ask the members of each group to devise a whimsical name for their group. What follows is one possible scenario.

Three days with Ms. Johnson

Time: The beginning of a ninth-grade mathematics lesson, several weeks into the year.

Day 1

1. Ms. Johnson says, "Over the past few weeks I have noticed that many of you have different and interesting ways of solving problems. I thought you would find it enjoyable and informative to exchange some ideas regarding the homework. So today, instead of going over the homework in the usual way, let's try something new! Why don't you all take out your work and arrange yourselves in groups of about four each."

2. After the students are seated in groups, Ms. Johnson says, "Now discuss your ideas and see if you can arrive at a set of solutions that you, as a group, believe makes sense. When you have finished, hand in the solutions that you have agreed on, and we will have a class discussion about the work."

3. When all the group papers have been submitted, Ms. Johnson engages the class in a discussion about those solutions on which the students couldn't agree.

4. Ms. Johnson says, "Tonight I will read your group papers, and tomorrow I will give you feedback on your group work. Since I will need a way to refer to each group, please have a group meeting before tomorrow and agree on a name for your group. I hope you had fun doing this because I know I really enjoyed hearing you discuss mathematics together. Please write a journal entry letting me know your feelings about working in a group. We'll discuss this tomorrow before we do group work again."

Day 2

1. Each group submits its name and a list of members.

2. Ms. Johnson returns the group papers from the previous day and announces how well each group did. She engages the students in a discussion about those problems that she or the students think need additional clarification.

3. Students form their groups and agree on the homework due for that day.

4. Ms. Johnson walks around the room checking that the students are prepared with their work, are participating in the group's discussions, and are helping one another understand the work.

5. Each group submits one set of solutions.

6. Ms. Johnson leads a discussion about problems requested by the students or about those that some groups found difficult.

7. The class members spend a few minutes discussing their reactions to working in groups. They are asked to focus on ways that they might benefit from such group work.

8. Ms. Johnson continues with the activities she has planned for the class.

9. In addition to the mathematics homework, students write a journal entry describing the help they gave or received when they worked in their groups today.

Day 3

1. Ms. Johnson displays a chart with the team names and members.

2. She explains the scoring procedure, which uses a tally system. The groups are ranked for the day on the basis of the number of correct solutions they have on the assignment. The group with the most correct solutions is ranked first and receives 1 point; the team with the second highest number of correct solutions is ranked second and receives 2 points. Tying teams receive the same number of points.

3. Ms. Johnson returns the previous day's group work, announcing the group's name, the group's rank on that assignment, and the new cumulative score from the past two days. At the end of a unit, the group with the *lowest* cumulative score is considered the most successful group.

Discussion

The scenario given above demonstrates one way that groups can be used to review homework. Note that it is not necessary to discuss all the assigned work. Often only the most challenging homework need be discussed with the whole class. At other times the teacher may wish to single out those problems that are most suitable for group or class discussion because they illustrate a particular idea or method. Other solutions can be made available or discussed at the students' request.

In a brief, three-day period, Ms. Johnson has given her students the opportunity to work in small groups in an environment that values cooperation as a means of success. When students can check their homework in the privacy of the group, trivial difficulties can be resolved within the group. The whole class does not have to direct its attention to these issues. While the students participate in their groups, the teacher is free to give individual attention where it is needed. The teacher may check a student's work, ask a question, pinpoint a student's difficulties, or make suggestions that will help a student develop behaviors needed to work effectively with others.

Having the groups discuss their homework, work that each student has done individually, maximizes the probability that each student will have something to contribute to the group. Students who work together depend on one another in a very positive sense. Each student depends on all the other group members to do the homework and to do a good job on it. Knowing that they must achieve as a group encourages students to support their peers' academic achievement.

Ms. Johnson's students have had the opportunity to discuss mathematics with one another in a small-group setting. They have worked together in a pleasant, nonthreatening environment, and they have all benefited. By talking about mathematics with one another, students have learned mathematics *and* acquired some of the skills needed to work cooperatively. They have begun to see how cooperative learning can enhance their own individual learning.

The following section discusses many other opportunities to use cooperative learning in the mathematics class. It also refers to examples of cooperative learning activities that appear at the end of the book.

Other Opportunities for Cooperative Learning in the Mathematics Class

Homework Review (Another Approach)

Groups can be used to review homework. For example, the teacher may wish to have particular problems or applications demonstrated at the chalkboard. Each group can be held responsible for discussing one problem that they have agreed on. One member of the group can write the solution on the board while another student, the spokesperson for the group, explains the group's work to the class. Since the teacher chooses the spokesperson and group members do not know who that will be, each student must be prepared to be that spokesperson. To add excitement to the class, the teacher can select group spokespersons at random. One way to do this is to assign each member of the group a number from 1 to 4. The teacher then rolls a tetrahedral die to determine which person from each group will be the spokesperson. After the spokesperson has presented the group's ideas, members of other groups can challenge the work or offer constructive criticism. Any group member can respond to such criticism by either accepting it or defending the group's original solution.

It is not unusual for certain groups to be more successful than others. To maintain the enjoyment and excitement of group work, the more challenging problems can be assigned to these groups. The teacher must be aware, however, that it is not just the groups with the highest scores that enjoy the challenge and prestige of more-difficult problems. All groups enjoy work that is both challenging and at their level of ability.

The Developmental Lesson

Cooperative learning is a versatile approach at many different points in the lesson for many different purposes. In the course of a developmental lesson, some new concept, technique, or generalization evolves.

Applying and practicing newly learned concepts. The teacher and students engage in discussion in which new ideas and techniques are developed, explained, and demonstrated. These techniques may be used for doing computation, solving equations, drawing graphs, proving theorems, and so on. Students need to apply their new knowledge so that they can see how well they understand the new concepts. Students are expected to ask questions about the work so that the class can engage in a discussion that will help clarify any misunderstandings the students may have. Unfortunately, in a whole-class setting, students are often reluctant to ask questions. They fear the embarrassment of being wrong or appearing ignorant.

Small-group work offers a good setting in which students can apply their knowledge and practice their new skills. In this approach, problems are assigned and the students are given time to work on them *individually*. Instead of being called together for a whole-class discussion, the students meet in groups to discuss and agree on their work. Each group hands in one copy of the solutions agreed on. After the work has been submitted, the teacher leads a discussion of those applications needing further clarification. Having discussed the problems in their groups, students are eager to clear up any misunderstandings.

As an added assignment, the group may be asked to respond to two questions: What have we learned today that we didn't know before? and What would we like to know as a result of today's work? The two suggested questions allow each group to summarize the new concepts they learned and give the teacher ideas for future work. Educators have discovered advantages to having students write in all subjects. Asking the groups to write a sentence or two about what they have learned on a particular day helps the students reflect on their work. It can help them integrate new ideas into their previous knowledge and see how each new idea fits into the whole mathematical picture. It may also suggest what is still to come or what they still don't know. Students who participate in stimulating small-group discussions begin to assume some responsibility for their own learning.

See Activities 4, 5, 10, 11, and 12 for examples of cooperative learning activities that apply concepts.

Guided discovery. A developmental lesson designed for guided discovery leading to concept development or mathematical generalizations suits cooperative-learning well. Each member of a group can be assigned a different task. After completing their different assignments, group members record their results on a group record sheet. When appropriate, they may look for a pattern. The group constructs a general statement that describes their results. For example, a group may be given a set of triangles in different shapes and sizes. They are to measure the angles of each triangle. Each student receives a protractor and several different triangles to measure: obtuse, isosceles, equilateral, scalene, and right triangles. Some are small and some are large. After each student has recorded the measurements of his or her triangles, the group meets to record and discuss the results. They try to discern a pattern in their collected data. They agree on a general statement about *all* triangles. Once these statements have been written on an overhead-projector transparency or on the chalkboard, the class compares and discusses the statements. The teacher guides the class until they agree on the generalized statement that culminates the day's lesson.

This approach has a number of advantages. Since each student is responsible to the group to do his or her own piece of the work, all group members will be actively involved in the group's work. Dividing up the work this way saves valuable class time; the group gathers more data in less time. The group members are using inductive reasoning and practicing behaviors that enhance their problem-solving skills. They are also learning that cooperation pays off.

Technology has made the guided-discovery approach more viable, since it allows quicker and often more-accurate explorations. Its ease of use facilitates the examination of more cases and leads to easier detection of patterns. For example, students can use graphing calculators to notice patterns in graphs and their related equations. Other applications of technology in the cooperative learning setting can be found in Anderson (1988), Male (1990), Male et al. (1987), McDonald (1989), and Sheets and Heid (1990).

See Activities 2, 6, 7, 8, 9, 13, and 15 for examples of cooperative learning activities using guided discovery.

The Review Lesson

The small-group setting is particularly suitable for review and reinforcement, which can be done in a manner similar to the one explained above for homework review or with practice problems related to newly developed concepts. Review and reinforcement can also be done in the form of a game.

Team mathematics bee. The team mathematics bee is a variation of the classic spelling bee. Each group is a team competing for the class championship. Teams are numbered 1, 2, 3, …. The teacher presents the same problem to each team. Team 1 responds to the problem. A spokesperson for the group, chosen by the teacher, explains the team's solution. The team receives 1 point for a correct solution and 1 point for a proper explanation. If the team receives fewer than 2 points, then Team 2 offers a different solution, explanation, or both, as needed. They then receive the appropriate points. Each team, in order, presents its solution or explanation until both a correct solution and explanation have been presented. The teacher then gives the groups another problem to consider. The next team (after the one that solved or gave the correct solution to the previous problem) gets the first chance to respond to the new problem. The process continues until the groups have worked on all the review problems. Time should be allowed for discussing questions and clarifying ideas. At the end of the game, the team with the most points is declared the champion. It is not only the champion group, however, that has won. All students will have put effort into an enjoyable review lesson, and each student will have benefited.

This review technique can be enhanced further if the review questions are composed of problems that the teams have submitted in advance as troublesome or worthy of review. Furthermore, this game will be most effective when it is structured carefully. When students are given a problem that they must work on in a group, the potential exists for some students to sit back and let others do the work. This is less likely to happen if each student has had the opportunity to work on the problem before the group discusses it. It is important for students to realize that every team member must be able to discuss the team's solution, since the teacher may choose any one of them to be the spokesperson. The prospect of having to explain the solution to the class means that students must help one another understand each problem and work together on solving it. Cooperation becomes an important method for achieving group success.

Challenge mathematics bee. A variation of the team mathematics bee is the challenge mathematics bee. In this game, the teacher does not determine whether or not a solution or explanation is correct. Instead, after one team presents its solution and explanation, the next team, in order, can challenge the solution, the explanation, or both. If a team challenges a solution and is correct, that team receives 2 points. If a team challenges a correct solution, however, the team with the correct solution gets 2 points. The same holds for challenging an explanation. Once again, the teacher selects the spokesperson for each team. If the second team does not wish to challenge, that opportunity passes on to each subsequent team. If there are no challenges, the first team receives 1 point. In this game students are given more responsibility for their own learning. It is the students, not the teacher, who decide which solutions and explanations are correct. Their attention level is high, and students soon learn that success depends on cooperation within the group.

See Activity 14 for an example of a cooperative review. The questions listed may be assigned the previous night for homework or individually to the groups on the day of the review and used for a mathematics bee.

Test Review

A sample test can be assigned for homework. The students then meet in groups to discuss the test and deepen their understanding of the concepts and techniques that will be assessed. By working on the sample test individually, each student comes to the group discussion with an accurate picture of his or her understanding. Students can prepare themselves and other group members for the forthcoming test. Each student is glad to participate in the review so that he or she will do well on the test. Once again, each group agrees on the solutions to the problems and submits one group paper. The teacher allows time for the whole class to discuss areas that need clarification.

Enrichment

Mathematics educators are realizing more than ever the important role that enrichment activities play in the mathematics program (NCTM 1989). When enrichment is an integral part of their work in mathematics, students of all ages and abilities learn to appreciate mathematics as a living, useful, interesting subject.

Students want to know how mathematics is used in various careers, in the world around them, in the stock market, in the supermarket, or in the daily newspaper. They are proud to learn that their ancestors (men, women, Hispanics, African Americans, etc.) have made important contributions to the development of mathematics and that people of their own background are making contributions right now. They are interested in seeing how mathematics is involved in music, art, and the sciences. For many students, intriguing problems or puzzles not only offer exciting sources of recreation but also spark their interest in mathematics.

See Activity 1 for an example of cooperative learning that calls for students to see the role of numbers in real life.

Historical topics. Group work is an excellent way of incorporating enrichment experiences into the mathematics class. To spark student interest in a new topic, cooperative learning groups can investigate the topic's historical development.

The members of the group should divide up the work. One student looks up the dateline in the topic's development. Another student researches the mathematicians who helped develop the topic. The group will want to have a person look for anecdotes and events related to the topic. Finally, a group member can investigate how this topic has affected the world as it is today. The group project might culminate in a bulletin board display or a written or oral report.

Statistical projects. In a class studying statistics, each group can conduct a survey that answers a question or deals with an issue of interest to students in the class or school. Each group collects data and records them in tables. They study the data and display them in graphs. Computer programs or graphing calculators can be used for data entry and display as well. Finally, each group interprets its data and reports its findings to the whole class. There is much to be done, and the group members must cooperate to accomplish the task. Individuals will work on their own some of the time, for there will have to be a division of labor. When all the pieces come together, however, it will be the group that gets credit for the final product.

See Activity 3 for an example of a cooperative learning survey project.

Recreational mathematics. Cooperative learning groups can engage in recreational mathematics that may not relate to current classwork. Such activities can take the form of puzzles, games, or problems that challenge the students to do creative problem solving. This work can be organized in many different ways. For example, on Monday the teacher posts one problem-solving activity on the bulletin board. The groups try to solve the problem by the end of the week. At the end of the week those groups that claim to have solved the problem present their solutions. The teacher chooses a spokesperson for a group. The spokesperson must present the group's solution satisfactorily before the group can get credit for solving the problem. The teacher could also have a grab bag of problems: each group selects a different activity. Again, the group gets credit for a solution only if the spokesperson selected by the teacher can explain the work with clarity and understanding.

Group problem solving has many advantages. Group members engage in brainstorming, an activity that enables all members to participate in the free flow of ideas. The cooperative learning atmosphere can be a secure environment for everyone to make a contribution. The student who is poor at solving problems can participate in the problem-solving process along with more able peers. Not only do all students learn how to solve problems, but they also share the excitement when the problem has been solved.

The cooperative learning literature sets forth many other strategies that researchers have developed and studied. Recently, teachers and researchers in the field have recognized that a combination of strategies is often most suitable for achieving the goals of a lesson. Below is a summary of some of the most well-known strategies.

Other Cooperative Learning Schemes

Slavin (1980b) developed and studied several methods he calls Student Team Learning. In one method, Student Teams Achievement Divisions (STAD), the teacher presents a lesson, and the students then meet in teams of four or five to complete a set of worksheets on the lesson. Each student then takes a quiz on the material. The scores the students contribute to their teams are based on the degree to which they have improved over their individual past averages. The highest-scoring teams are recognized in a weekly class newsletter. Another method, Teams-Games-Tournament (TGT), is similar to STAD, but instead of taking quizzes, the students play academic games as their teams' representatives. They compete with other students having similar achievement levels.

In Jigsaw II, a modification of an earlier cooperative learning method by Aronson (1978), each team is the same set of special topics to investigate. The teams assign a topic to each member. After studying the topic individually, the students from different teams who were assigned the same topic meet to exchange ideas and information. The students then return to their own team to teach their teammates what they learned. The students take a quiz on the material, and their scores are used to form individual and team scores.

Johnson and Johnson (1991) support a cooperative learning technique they have named Learning Together. In this strategy, students meet in heterogeneous groups of four or five and work on assignment sheets. When the group agrees on solutions to the problems assigned, the entire group submits a single answer sheet. Recognition is based on the group product. Johnson and Johnson make it clear, however, that the following conditions must exist for group learning to take place: positive interdependence, face-to-face positive interaction, individual accountability, social skills, and group processing.

Other popular techniques are Group Investigation (Sharan and Hertz-Lazarowitz 1980) and Co-op Co-op (Kagan 1985), which are similar in that they are both oriented toward complex, multifaceted learning tasks and give students more control of what and how to learn. Andrini (1996) promotes other strategies such as Numbered Heads Together, Think-Pair-Share, Pairs Check, and Round Table, each of which can be used to promote individual accountability and meaningful intragroup communication.

Each of the cooperative learning schemes above has its advantages and disadvantages in different learning situations. It takes knowledge, experience, and sensitivity to know how to use the techniques to their best advantage.

CONCLUDING REMARKS

Cooperative learning has much to offer the mathematics class. Students enjoy discussing mathematics with other students; they benefit from interacting with their peers as well as with the teacher.

. In the traditional teacher-centered classroom, depicted in figure 1, the teacher is clearly at the center of all class activity. All lines of communication are between individual students and the teacher. In contrast, figure 2 depicts the cooperative learning classroom. Although the teacher still retains a central role, he or she is no longer responsible for all mathematical learning. Students help the teacher meet the demands of dealing with a whole class by serving as resources for one another within their groups.

Cooperative learning is a valuable instructional strategy for every teacher. It is hoped that enough has been presented here to help the teacher get started. Each teacher creates a cooperative learning classroom in his or her own way. In the process, the teacher will have to make many decisions about how to proceed. Each class is different, and what works for one may not work for another. The teacher in a cooperative learning class must be courageous, make choices, and dive right in! Adjustments and refinements can be made as the need arises.

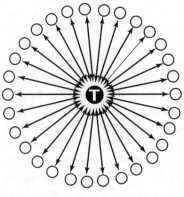

Fig. 1. Teacher-centered classroom

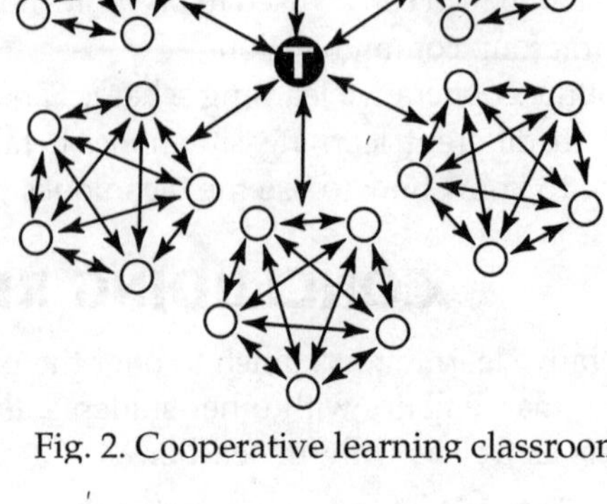

Fig. 2. Cooperative learning classroom

SAMPLE ACTIVITIES

The sample activities that follow illustrate some mathematics lessons that have been adapted for use with cooperative learning groups.

ACTIVITY 1: How Are Numbers Used in Our Lives?

Learning Level: Elementary school

Curriculum Area: Number categories; number sense

Objectives:

1. To become aware of numbers in the environment
2. To understand the different ways that numbers are used

Group Size: Three or four students

Materials for Each Group:

Problem sheets for each student
(or oral instructions by teacher)
Poster paper, scissors, glue, crayons
Old magazines and newspapers (for cutting)

Teaching Notes:

- Young children will need some help understanding what it is they are expected to do.
- Groups will need some help in seeing how numbers fall into categories according to the ways they are used: numbers for counting, identification, location, measurement, and order.
- You will want to give each group the opportunity to talk about its numbers and the way they are used. The posters will make fine additions to your bulletin board.

PROBLEM SHEET FOR ACTIVITY 1

How Are Numbers Used in Our Lives?

You will keep a Math Log for one week. Each day you will write in your log the numbers you see and the way each number is used. If possible, draw a picture, or cut out a picture from a newspaper or magazine that shows the way the number is used.

Bring in your log one week from today. You will meet with your group to discuss what you have found. The group should talk about the different ways that numbers are used. The group will then prepare a poster showing an example or a picture of each way that numbers are used.

ACTIVITY 2: What Is a Minute?

Learning Level: Elementary school

Curriculum Area: Measurement

Objectives:

1. To explore the concept of one minute
2. To experiment with the relationship between time and speed
3. To express speed as a number per minute

Group Size: Four students

Materials for Each Group:

   1 timing device

   Beads and thread

   1 ball

   4 problem sheets

   1 record chart sheet

   4 job cards: Timekeeper, Jumper, Bead Threader, Ball Bouncer

   1 pencil

Teaching Notes:

- If your classroom has a clock with a second hand, you can have your pupils sit quietly while the second hand sweeps around the clock for one minute.
- Young children may not be able to read the directions on their own. You need to be sure that each pupil understands what is to be done. It may be helpful to include one good reader in each group.
- Have a member of each group share the group's results with the class. Which is the activity that pupils can do the greatest number of times in one minute? Which is the activity that pupils do the smallest number of times in one minute?
- Have the groups give their ideas about things they can try to do in one minute. If possible, try some of them.

PROBLEM SHEET FOR ACTIVITY 2

What Is a Minute?

Before beginning the activity, each pupil draws a job card that tells who is the timekeeper, who is the jumper, who is the bead threader, and who is the ball bouncer. (Pupil jobs will switch in a little while.) Pupils write their names on a line of the record chart.

1. Each pupil should read aloud what he or she must do. The others should follow along silently while a pupil reads.

   Timekeeper: I am the timekeeper and recorder. I will tell the others when to start. At the end of one minute, I will tell them to stop. I will write each pupil's results in the chart.

   Jumper: When the timekeeper tells me to start, I will jump up and down and count the number of times I can jump up and down in one minute.

   Bead Threader: When the timekeeper tells me to start, I will thread beads and count the number of beads I can thread in one minute.

   Ball Bouncer: When the timekeeper tells me to start, I will bounce the ball and count the number of times I can bounce the ball in one minute.

   After the minute has ended, the timekeeper should record each pupil's count on the correct line of the record chart.

2. Pupils switch jobs with another member of the group. Each person should do something different from what he or she did before. When one minute is over, the pupil who is now timekeeper should enter each count in the record chart.

3. Switch jobs and repeat the counting activities until each pupil has done each activity once. All counts should now be in the record chart.

4. After all the results are in the record chart, talk about the results. Which is the activity that pupils can do the greatest number of times in one minute? Which is the activity that pupils do the smallest number of times in one minute?

See if your group can agree on four other things you can try to do in one minute. Write them down on the record chart sheet.

RECORD CHART SHEET FOR ACTIVITY 2

Record Chart

Pupil's Name	Number of Jumps per Minute	Number of Beads per Minute	Number of Bounces per Minute

Other Things to Try to Do in One Minute

1. _____

_____

2. _____

_____

3. _____

_____

4. _____

_____

ACTIVITY 3: Food Preferences for Students

Learning Level: Elementary school

Curriculum Area: Statistics, problem solving, fractions

Objectives:

1. To organize data in table form
2. To select appropriate data for solving problems
3. To use sample data to make predictions
4. To work with fractions using real data

Group Size: Three or four students

Materials for Each Group:

   1 problem sheet with record chart

   (each group gets a different problem sheet)

   1 envelope containing student answers to one class survey question

Teaching Notes:

- Have each student in the class fill out and hand in a copy of the survey form that follows the problem sheets for this activity. There should be enough questions on the form so that each group can tabulate and analyze the data for at least one question.

- When the survey forms have been collected, separate the questions. Place all student answers to question 1 in an envelope for group 1, answers to question 2 in an envelope for group 2, answers to question 3 in an envelope for group 3, and so on.

- When the groups have tabulated and analyzed the answers to the survey questions, each group will share its results and conclusions with the whole class.

PROBLEM SHEET FOR ACTIVITY 3

Food Preferences for Students (Question 1)

Your group has been given question 1 from the class's food preference survey to analyze.

Take turns!

1. One student should read the answer from each sheet. Another student should tally the results on the record sheet.

2. Total the number of tallies in each box of the table.

3. Find the totals across the bottom row. Discuss what each total means.

4. Find the totals in the last column. What does each total mean?

5. Discuss each question below and agree on an answer for each one.

   a) What fraction of the girls prefer chocolate ice cream?

   Answer_____

   b) What fraction of the students who prefer chocolate ice cream are girls?

   Answer_____

   c) What fraction of the students are girls who prefer chocolate ice cream?

   Answer_____

   d)Use the data in your table to estimate the number of boys in your grade who prefer vanilla ice cream. (Assume that there are 200 students in your grade.)

   Answer_____

Record Chart (Question 1)

	Vanilla	Chocolate	Strawberry	Total
Boys				
Girls				
Total				

PROBLEM SHEET FOR ACTIVITY 3

Food Preferences for Students (Question 2)

Your group has been given question 2 from the class's food preference survey to analyze.

Take turns!

1. One student should read the answer from each sheet. Another student should tally the results on the record sheet.

2. Total the number of tallies in each box of the table.

3. Find the totals across the bottom row. Discuss what each total means.

4. Find the totals in the last column. What does each total mean?

5. Discuss each question below and agree on an answer for each one.

   a) What fraction of the boys prefer hamburgers for lunch?

   Answer_____
   b) What fraction of the students who prefer hamburgers for lunch are boys?

   Answer_____
   c) What fraction of the students are boys who prefer hamburgers for lunch?

   Answer_____
   d) Use the data in your table to estimate the number of girls in your grade who prefer frankfurters for lunch. (Assume that there are 200 students in your grade.)

   Answer_____

Record Chart (Question 2)

	Frankfurter	Hamburger	Pizza	Total
Boys				
Girls				
Total				

PROBLEM SHEET FOR ACTIVITY 3

Food Preferences for Students (Question 3)

Your group has been given question 3 from the class's food preference survey to analyze.

Take turns!

1. One student should read the answer from each sheet. Another student should tally the results on the record sheet.

2. Total the number of tallies in each box of the table.

3. Find the totals across the bottom row. Discuss what each total means.

4. Find the totals in the last column. What does each total mean?

5. Discuss each question below and agree on an answer for each one.

   a) What fraction of the girls prefer carrots as a vegetable?

       Answer_____

   b) What fraction of the students who prefer carrots as a vegetable are girls?

       Answer_____

   c) What fraction of the students are girls who prefer carrots as a vegetable?

       Answer_____

   d) Use the data in your table to estimate the number of boys in your grade who prefer peas as a vegetable. (Assume that there are 200 students in your grade.)

       Answer_____

Record Chart (Question 3)

	Carrots	Cauliflower	Peas	Total
Girls				
Boys				
Total				

PROBLEM SHEET FOR ACTIVITY 3

Food Preferences for Students (Question 4)

Your group has been given question 4 from the class's food preference survey to analyze.

Take turns!

1. One student should read the answer from each sheet. Another student should tally the results on the record sheet.

2. Total the number of tallies in each box of the table.

3. Find the totals across the bottom row. Discuss what each total means.

4. Find the totals in the last column. What does each total mean?

5. Discuss each question below and agree on an answer for each one.

   a) What fraction of the boys prefer soda as a drink?

   Answer _____

   b) What fraction of the students who prefer soda as a drink are boys?

   Answer _____

   c) What fraction of the students are boys who prefer soda as a drink?

   Answer _____

   d) Use the data in your table to estimate the number of girls in your grade who prefer milk as a drink. (Assume that there are 200 students in your grade.)

   Answer _____

Record Chart (Question 4)

	Apple Juice	Milk	Soda	Total
Boys				
Girls				
Total				

PROBLEM SHEET FOR ACTIVITY 3

Food Preferences for Students (Question 5)

Your group has been given question 5 from the class's food preference survey to analyze.

Take turns!

1. One student should read the answer from each sheet. Another student should tally the results on the record sheet.

2. Total the number of tallies in each box of the table.

3. Find the totals across the bottom row. Discuss what each total means.

4. Find the totals in the last column. What does each total mean?

5. Discuss each question below and agree on an answer for each one.

   a) What fraction of the girls prefer Burger King's food?

   Answer _____

   b) What fraction of the students who prefer Burger King's food are girls?

   Answer _____

   c) What fraction of the students are girls who prefer Burger King's food?

   Answer _____

   d) Use the data in your table to estimate the number of boys in your grade who prefer McDonald's food. (Assume that there are 200 students in your grade.)

   Answer _____

Record Chart (Question 5)

	Burger King	McDonald's	Wendy's	Total
Girls				
Boys				
Total				

PROBLEM SHEET FOR ACTIVITY 3

Food Preferences for Students (Question 6)

Your group has been given question 6 from the class's food preference survey to analyze.

Take turns!

1. One student should read the answer from each sheet. Another student should tally the results on the record sheet.

2. Total the number of tallies in each box of the table.

3. Find the totals across the bottom row. Discuss what each total means.

4. Find the totals in the last column. What does each total mean?

5. Discuss each question below and agree on an answer for each one.

   a) What fraction of the boys prefer fruit as a snack?

   Answer_____

   b) What fraction of the students who prefer fruit as a snack are boys?

   Answer_____

   c) What fraction of the students are boys who prefer fruit as a snack?

   Answer_____

   d) Use the data in your table to estimate the number of girls in your grade who prefer pretzels as a snack. (Assume that there are 200 students in your grade.)

   Answer_____

Record Chart (Question 6)

	Fruit	Potato chips	Pretzels	Total
Boys				
Girls				
Total				

SURVEY FORM FOR ACTIVITY 3

Food Preferences of Students

Directions: Answer each question by checking only one box. Be sure to indicate whether you are a boy or a girl *for each question.*

1. Which ice cream flavor do you like best?

   ☐ Chocolate   ☐ Strawberry   ☐ Vanilla

   Are you a boy or a girl?   ☐ Boy   ☐ Girl

2. Which lunch do you like best?

   ☐ Frankfurter   ☐ Hamburger   ☐ Pizza

   Are you a boy or a girl?   ☐ Boy   ☐ Girl

3. Which vegetable do you like best?

   ☐ Carrots   ☐ Cauliflower   ☐ Peas

   Are you a boy or a girl?   ☐ Boy   ☐ Girl

4. Which drink do you like best?

   ☐ Apple juice   ☐ Milk   ☐ Soda

   Are you a boy or a girl?   ☐ Boy   ☐ Girl

5. Which restaurant's food do you like best?

   ☐ Burger King   ☐ McDonald's   ☐ Wendy's

   Are you a boy or a girl?   ☐ Boy   ☐ Girl

6. Which snack do you like best?

   ☐ Fruit   ☐ Potato chips   ☐ Pretzels

   Are you a boy or a girl?   ☐ Boy   ☐ Girl

ACTIVITY 4: Estimation with Money

Learning Level: Elementary school

Curriculum Area: Estimation, money, geometry

Objectives:

1. To appreciate how estimation can be used in place of computation
2. To use various methods of estimation with money
3. To learn a systematic method of recording data
4. To develop concepts of geometry

Group Size: Three students

Materials for Each Group:

   3 problem sheets

   1 record chart sheet

   1 calculator (to be retained by the teacher until the group hands in its
      results)

Teaching Notes:

• Appoint a reader and a recorder for each group.

• When a group has handed in its list, you may wish to give that group a calculator so that the members can calculate the exact cost of each purchase.

• You may wish to appoint a group spokesperson to report the group's methods
   and results to the class.

PROBLEM SHEET FOR ACTIVITY 4

Estimation with Money

One person should read the instructions while the other group members follow along. When the reader has completed the reading, the group members should discuss what they must do.

Instructions:

1. Your group has $10 to spend. What can you buy?

    Rules: a) You must buy at least three items.

    b) You may buy more than one of an item.

    c) You may spend any amount of money—up to $10—in any way you wish.

2. Work together to list the items that your group could buy. One person should record the items on the record chart.

3. The recorder should list as many different combinations of items as the group can find. Use *estimation,* not computation, because it is faster! Show the approximate total cost of each combination of items on the record chart.

4. Hand in your group record when you are finished. KEEP A COPY OF WHAT YOU HAND IN!

RECORD CHART SHEET FOR ACTIVITY 4

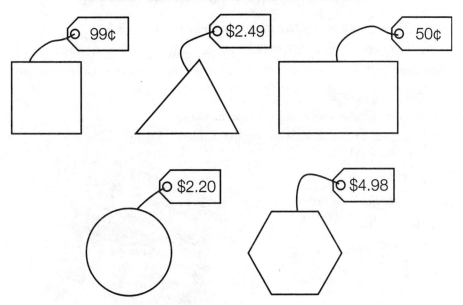

Record Chart

Purchase Number	Items Purchased	Approximate Cost of Purchase
1.		
2.		
3.		
4.		
5.		
6.		
7.		
8.		
9.		
10.		

ACTIVITY 5: Problem Solving Using Division and the Calculator

Learning Level: Elementary and middle school

Curriculum Area: Problem solving

Objectives:

1. To analyze problems
2. To use the calculator as a tool in problem solving
3. To practice the relationships among the dividend, the divisor, the quotient, and the remainder

Group Size: Four students

Materials for Each Group:

　　4 problem sheets

　　1 calculator

Teaching Notes:

• Students should practice writing the relationships among the dividend, divisor, quotient, and remainder before engaging in this activity.

• Students should practice using a calculator to compute the quotient and *whole-number* remainder.

　　Example:　After entering 35 ÷ 8 = , note that the display shows 4.375. The whole-number part of the quotient is 4. The decimal means there is a remainder. The whole-number remainder, r, is computed by using $r = 35 - (8 \times 4)$.

• In some cases, the answer to a problem will be the whole-number quotient. In other cases it will be the quotient plus 1. In some cases it will be sufficient to know that there is a remainder. In other cases it will be necessary to compute the whole-number remainder.

• The teacher may want to alert students to the fact that it is often necessary to pay sales tax on purchases or pay interest on delayed payments.

• A group gets credit for the correct solution only if any person called on in the group presents a correct explanation of the problem to the class.

PROBLEM SHEET FOR ACTIVITY 5

Problem Solving Using Division and the Calculator

All of the problems in this activity are to be solved by using a calculator to obtain information without pencil-and-paper computation. All problems involve division. However, the students in your group must analyze each problem to decide how the division results should be used to solve the problem.

TAKE TURNS USING THE CALCULATOR! One student should read the problem while the others follow along. Discuss the problem. Then proceed with the calculation and the solution.

When the members of your group have agreed on the best solution for each problem, submit *one set* of solutions for your group. Each person must be able to explain any of the group's solutions to the whole class.

1. How many quarters can you exchange for 149 pennies?

2. A class of 302 students and 5 adults are going on a field trip by bus.

    a) If each bus holds 42 persons, how many buses will be needed?

    b) Once you have determined how many buses will be needed, decide how the people should be distributed on the buses. Will additional adults be needed so that there will be one adult on each bus?

3. There are 1226 candy bars and they are to be packed 24 to a box. How many boxes will be needed? Will there be any candy bars left over?

4. A class has $10.75 to spend on notebooks and pads. Notebooks cost 69 cents and pads cost 27 cents. How many notebooks can the pupils buy if they buy as many notebooks as possible? Will there be enough money left to buy any pads? If so, how many pads can they buy?

5. A computer store advertises that a computer that costs $899 (without tax) can be purchased by paying as little as $35 a month. Mr. Day decides to buy the computer and pay $55 a month. How long will it take him to pay for the computer? How much will his last payment be?

6. Suppose today is Monday. Will it be a Monday 2646 days from today?

ACTIVITY 6: Arrangements

Learning Level: Middle school or junior high school

Curriculum Area: Permutations

Objectives:

1. To derive a formula for permutations by discerning a pattern
2. To use concrete materials as an aid to reasoning

Group Size: Four students

Materials for Each Group:

    4 problem sheets
    1 record sheet for coloring squares
    5 different-colored cube blocks (same size)
    5 different-colored crayons, matching the cube colors

Teaching Notes:

- It is hoped that students will see that there are four positions for the fourth block once a three-block arrangement is in place. That is, given the following three-block arrangement,

R	B	G

W

a white block can be placed as shown.

Thus, each three-block arrangement yields 4 *four-block* arrangements.

- There are 2 two-block arrangements, 3 • 2, or 6, three-block arrangements, and 4 • 3 • 2, or 24, four-block arrangements.

- The same line of reasoning means that a fifth block can be placed in five positions

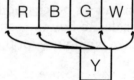

so that there are 5 • 4 • 3 • 2, or 120, different arrangements of five blocks.

PROBLEM SHEET FOR ACTIVITY 6

Arrangements

1. There are two ways to place two blocks in a row. Take turns! Place a red block and a blue block in a row. Use red and blue crayons to color the interiors of two squares to look like the blocks.

Rearrange the blocks and color the squares another way.

2. How many ways can three blocks be placed in a row?
Use three different-colored blocks. Take turns!

   a) Arrange the three blocks in a row.

   b) Color squares on the record sheet to show each arrangement.

   c) How many arrangements are there?

3. How many ways can four blocks be arranged in a row?
Make four-block arrangements from each three-block arrangement. Share the work! Work in pairs! Take turns!

   a) Make *one* of the three-block arrangements.

   (1) Now take a fourth block of a different color and make a four-block arrangement from the three-block arrangement.

   (2) Color squares to show this four-block arrangement.

   (3) Move the fourth block to make a different four-block arrangement. Color squares to show this arrangement.

   (4) Make as many four-block arrangements as you can from the same three-block arrangement. Keep a record by coloring squares on your record sheet.

   (5) How many four-block arrangements have you made?

   b) Make four-block arrangements from each three-block arrangement. Keep a record by coloring squares.

   c) Discuss your findings with your teammates. Is there a pattern? How many four-block arrangements are there altogether?

4. How many five-block arrangements are there?
First you must agree on an easy way to solve this problem. Then answer the question.

RECORD CHART SHEET FOR ACTIVITY 6

Three-block arrangements

Four-block arrangements

ACTIVITY 7: Least Common Multiple and Greatest Common Factor

Learning Level: Junior high school

Curriculum Area: Number theory

Objectives:

1. To practice the computation of the least common multiple and greatest common factor
2. To derive the relationships among the least common multiple, the greatest common factor, and the product of the two numbers
3. To record data systematically
4. To discern a pattern by analyzing data

Group Size: Four students

Materials for Each Group:

4 problem sheets
1 record sheet
1 number envelope containing 12 slips of paper, each with a pair of numbers

Teaching Notes:

- Appoint a reader and a recorder for each group.
- If you decide to have a group report its findings to the entire class, choose a spokesperson for the group after all record sheets have been submitted.
- These are pairs of numbers (m, n) that are relatively prime; that is, 1 is the greatest common factor: (1, 3), (2, 3), (3, 5), (4, 7), (6, 11), (8, 15), (6, 35), (13, 17), (3, 46), (15, 26), (21, 5)
- These pairs of numbers (m, n) have a common factor greater than 1: (3, 6), (6, 8), (8, 12), (12, 26), (12, 15), (10, 12), (30, 45), (3, 645), (15, 65)

PROBLEM SHEET FOR ACTIVITY 7

Least Common Multiple and Greatest Common Factor

One person should read the instructions while other group members follow along. When the reader has completed the reading, others may question or explain the tasks and the requirements of the problem. When the group is ready to begin, each member should select, at random, three slips of paper from the number envelope.

1. Each person will receive three pairs of numbers. Analyze each pair of numbers, (m, n), to determine—

   a). the greatest common factor of m and n: GCF (m, n);
   b) the least common multiple of m and n: LCM (m, n);
   c) the product of m and n: $m \cdot n$.
   Example: GCF $(4, 6) = 2$, LCM $(4, 6) = 12$, $m \cdot n = 24$.

2. Each group member who has completed his or her part of the work should offer to help another member.

3. Students who have completed their work should exchange papers and check one another's results.

4. When all pairs of numbers have been analyzed, the recorder should list all group results on the record sheet.

5. When the group has agreed on the results, the members should discuss their findings and determine the relationships among the greatest common factor, the least common multiple, and the product of any two numbers.

6. State the relationship. Then test it out on four new pairs of numbers, one pair chosen by each group member.

7. The recorder should record the group's work in #6 on the record sheet. When the group has agreed on what is written on the record sheet, hand it in.

RECORD SHEET FOR ACTIVITY 7

Number Pairs (m, n)	GCF (m, n)	LCM (m, n)	Product ($m \cdot n$)

Relationship:

ACTIVITY 8: Properties of Parallelograms

Learning Level: Junior high school or secondary school

Curriculum Area: Geometry

Objectives:

1. To review the definitions of parallelogram, rectangle, rhombus, and square
2. To practice using a protractor to measure angles
3. To discern a pattern among the opposite angles of a parallelogram
4. To discern a pattern among the opposite sides of a parallelogram

Group Size: Four students

Materials for Each Group:

  4 problem sheets
  1 set of parallelogram sheets
  1 summary record sheet
  4 rulers
  4 protractors

Teaching Notes:

• One student in each group should read the Problem Sheet to the group while the others follow along.

• One student in each group should record the measurements and the *relationship statements* on the summary record sheet.

• If you wish to have a group report to the whole class, make a random selection of a student who will be the spokesperson for the group.

• A follow-up activity might involve the diagonals of the parallelogram.

PROBLEM SHEET FOR ACTIVITY 8

Properties of Parallelograms

There are four different parallelograms. Your group is to measure the sides and the angles of each one.

1. Split up the work! Each student should start with one parallelogram. Measure one side and one angle of the parallelogram. Be sure to record your measurements directly on the parallelogram sheet in the space provided.

2. Pass your sheet to another student in your group who will measure *one* side and *one* angle and record the measurements on the sheet.

3. Continue exchanging parallelograms until all measurements have been made.

4. Once all parallelograms have been measured, take turns dictating the information to the recorder, who will record it on the summary record sheet. If a particular measurement is challenged, the measurement should be made again in the presence of the other group members.

5. Once the group members agree on the data that have been entered on the summary record sheet, examine the data to see whether any patterns appear. Is there a relationship between particular sides of all parallelograms? Is there a relationship between particular angles of all parallelograms?

6. When you have completed the summary record sheet, hand it in.

PARALLELOGRAM SHEET FOR ACTIVITY 8

I

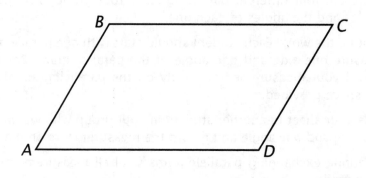

AB = _____	BC = _____
CD = _____	DA = _____
m∠A = _____	m∠B = _____
m∠C = _____	m∠D = _____

PARALLELOGRAM SHEET FOR ACTIVITY 8

||

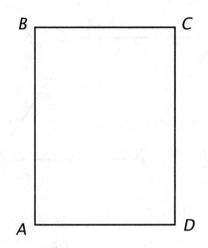

$AB =$ _____ $BC =$ _____

$CD =$ _____ $DA =$ _____

$m\angle A =$ _____ $m\angle B =$ _____

$m\angle C =$ _____ $m\angle D =$ _____

PARALLELOGRAM SHEET FOR ACTIVITY 8

III

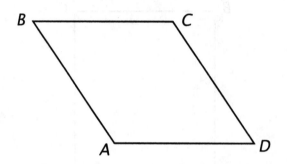

$AB =$ _____ $BC =$ _____

$CD =$ _____ $DA =$ _____

$m\angle A =$ _____ $m\angle B =$ _____

$m\angle C =$ _____ $m\angle D =$ _____

PARALLELOGRAM SHEET FOR ACTIVITY 8

IV

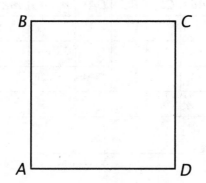

$AB =$ _____ $BC =$ _____

$CD =$ _____ $DA =$ _____

$m\angle A =$ _____ $m\angle B =$ _____

$m\angle C =$ _____ $m\angle D =$ _____

SUMMARY RECORD SHEET FOR ACTIVITY 8

Measurements

Parallelogram	AB	CD	BC	DA	$m\angle A$	$m\angle B$	$m\angle C$	$m\angle D$
I								
II								
III								
IV								

Relationship (sides) _____

Relationship (angles) _____

ACTIVITY 9: Coin-Die Experiment

Learning Level: Junior high school or secondary school

Curriculum Area: Probability

Objectives:

1. To conduct a probability experiment and record the results
2. To use the relative frequency definition of probability
3. To determine the mathematical probability of a compound event
4. To compare the relative frequency and mathematical probability of an event

Group Size: Three students

Materials for Each Group:

   3 problem sheets
   1 record sheet
   1 coin
   1 die

Teaching Notes:

- The 12 possible outcomes of the experiment appear on the record sheet. However, you may wish to discuss the fact that this number can be computed by using the multiplication principle: that is, 2×6.

- If your students are more advanced, you may wish them to construct their own record sheet.

PROBLEM SHEET FOR ACTIVITY 9

Coin-Die Experiment

One student should read through the instructions while the others follow along. Discuss the problem before proceeding.

For this experiment a trial is a toss of the coin and a roll of the die. Your group is to record the results of 50 trials on the accompanying record sheet.

1. One student should roll the die while a second student tosses the coin. The third student should tally the results on the record sheet.

2. After 25 trials, change roles.

3. Now that you have completed the experiment, answer the following questions:

   a) Experimental Probability

   (1) Use the relative frequency definition of probability to determine the probability of both a 5 and tails occurring.

   $P(5, T) = $ _____

   (2) If your group were to conduct another 100 trials, approximately how many times would you expect to see a 5 and tails?

   _____

   b) Mathematical Probability

   (1) How many outcomes are there for the compound event "roll a die and toss a coin"?

   _____

   (2) Are the outcomes equally likely?

   _____

   (3) What is the mathematical probability of both a 5 and tails occurring?

   $P(5, T) = $ _____

   c) Compare your results in parts *a* and *b* above. How could you change the experiment so that the result in part *a* is closer to the mathematical probability obtained in part *b*?

   _____

RECORD SHEET FOR ACTIVITY 9

Outcome	Tally	Frequency	Outcome	Tally	Frequency
(1, Heads)			(1, Tails)		
(2, Heads)			(2, Tails)		
(3, Heads)			(3, Tails)		
(4, Heads)			(4, Tails)		
(5, Heads)			(5, Tails)		
(6, Heads)			(6, Tails)		

ACTIVITY 10: Using Parentheses

Learning Level: Secondary school

Curriculum Area: Algebra

Objectives:

1. To use parentheses in the computation of numerical expressions
2. To use the "working backward" strategy to solve a problem

Group Size: Three or four students

Materials for Each Group:

    1 problem sheet

Teaching Notes:

• Students may try to solve these problems by using a trial-and-error placement of parentheses. Be sure the students are aware of the advantage of using a working-backward strategy.

• Select at random a member of each group to explain the group's solutions.

PROBLEM SHEET FOR ACTIVITY 10

Using Parentheses

The value of an expression depends on how parentheses are used.

1. Work together to place parentheses, when needed, to complete true statements.

$$2 + 3 \cdot 5^2 = 77$$

$$2 + 3 \cdot 5^2 = 125$$

$$2 + 3 \cdot 5^2 = 227$$

$$2 + 3 \cdot 5^2 = 289$$

2. Make up another set of problems similar to the ones given. Your teacher will give them to another group to solve.

3. When you have finished, hand in your group's work.

ACTIVITY 11: Probability with Linear Equations

Learning Level: Secondary school

Curriculum Area: Algebra, combinatorics, and probability

Objectives:

1. To apply permutations in the assignment of coefficients
2. To practice solving linear equations
3. To compute probabilities from a list of outcomes

Group Size: Three students

Materials for Each Group:

   1 problem sheet with record chart

Teaching Notes:

• Select at random one person from a group to explain the group's solution.

• The approach outlined for this topic can also be used in the activity "Probability with Quadratic Equations."

PROBLEM SHEET FOR ACTIVITY 11

Probability with Linear Equations

The numbers 2, 3, and 5 are substituted at random for p, q, and r in the equation $px + q = r$ ($p \neq q \neq r$).

- What is the probability that the solution is negative?
- What is the probability that the absolute value of the solution is 1?
- What is the probability that the solution is a fraction?
- If r is not 5, what is the probability that the solution is negative?

1. Engage in a group discussion of the problem and possible strategies for solution.

2. Work as a group to write down all the different possible substitutions of the numbers 2, 3, and 5 for p, q, and r. Use the record chart to record your results.

3. Complete the record chart by solving each equation. Be sure to divide the work so that each person in the group solves the same number of equations.

4. Compute each probability:

   a) Probability that the solution is negative

   _____

   b) Probability that the absolute value of the solution is 1

   _____

   c) Probability that the solution is a fraction

   _____

   d) Probability that the solution is negative when r is not 5

   _____

RECORD CHART FOR ACTIVITY 11

p	q	r	px + q = r	x

ACTIVITY 12: Probability with Quadratic Equations

Learning Level: Secondary school

Curriculum Area: Algebra, combinatorics, and probability

Objectives:

1. To apply permutations in the assignment of coefficients
2. To determine those values of the discriminant that allow the quadratic equation to be solved by factoring
3. To determine those values of the discriminant that produce real roots
4. To compute probabilities from a list of outcomes

Group Size: Three students

Materials for Each Group:

   1 problem sheet with record chart

Teaching Notes:

• Students should find that since there are six different permutations of a, b, and c, there are six different equations to consider.

PROBLEM SHEET FOR ACTIVITY 12

Probability with Quadratic Equations

The numbers 1, 3, and 4 are substituted at random for a, b, and c in the quadratic equation $ax^2 + bx + c = 0$ ($a \neq b \neq c$).

- What is the probability that $ax^2 + bx + c = 0$ can be solved by factoring?
- What is the probability that $ax^2 + bx + c = 0$ has real roots?

1. Engage in a group discussion of the problem and possible strategies for solution.

2. Work as a group to write down all the different possible substitutions of the numbers 1, 3, and 4 for a, b, and c. Use the record chart to record your results.

3. Complete the record chart by computing the discriminant for each equation.

4. Compute each probability.

   a) Probability that the equation can be solved by factoring

   _____

   b) Probability that the equation has real roots

   _____

RECORD CHART

a	b	c	$ax^2 + bx + c = 0$	$b^2 - 4ac$

ACTIVITY 13: Using Transformations to Graph Parabolas

Learning Level: Secondary school

Curriculum Area: Parabolas, transformation, geometry

Objectives:

1. To graph the parabola $y = x^2 + k$ (k a real number) by translating the graph of the parabola $y = x^2$

2. To graph the parabola $y = (x - h)^2$ (h a real number) by translating the graph of the parabola $y = x^2$

3. To graph the parabola $y = (x - h)^2 + k$ (h, k real numbers) by using a composition of translations of the parabola $y = x^2$

Group Size: Three students

Materials for Each Group:

   1 problem sheet
   Graph paper
   Tracing paper

Teaching Notes:

- Activity 1: To superimpose the graph of $y = x^2$ on the graphs of the form $y = x^2 + k$ (k a real number), the students must *translate* the graph $y = x^2$, k units in the direction of the y-axis.

- Activity 2: To superimpose the graph of $y = x^2$ on the graphs of the form $y = (x - h)^2$ (h a real number), the students must *translate* the graph $y = x^2$, h units in the direction of the x-axis.

- Activity 3: As a result of activities 1 and 2, the students will see that to obtain the graph of $y = (x - h)^2 + k$ (h, k real numbers) from the graph $y = x^2$, they must *translate* the graph $y = x^2$, k units in the direction of the y-axis and h units in the direction of the x-axis. The translation can be done in the reverse order as well.

PROBLEM SHEET FOR ACTIVITY 13

Using Transformations to Graph Parabolas

Exercise 1

1. On separate pieces of graph paper sketch the graph of each of the following equations:

    Student A: $y = x^2$
    Student B: $y = x^2 + 3$
    Student C: $y = x^2 - 4$

2. Student A: Use the tracing paper to trace your graph of $y = x^2$. Trace the axes as well.

3. In the group, use the tracing to discern a relationship among the three parabolas. Agree on the relationship, and write it in the space provided.

    Relationship: _____

    a) Place the tracing of the graph of $y = x^2$ on the graph of $y = x^2 + 3$ so that the *axes* coincide.

    Work together to state the transformation that can be used to obtain the graph of $y = x^2 + 3$ from the graph of $y = x^2$.

    Transformation: _____

    b) Place the tracing of the graph of $y = x^2$ on the graph of $y = x^2 - 4$ so that the *axes* coincide.

    State the transformation that can be used to obtain the graph of $y = x^2 - 4$ from the graph of $y = x^2$.

    Transformation: _____

4. Agree on a general method for obtaining the graph of $y = x^2 + k$ (k a real number) from the graph of $y = x^2$.

    Generalization: _____

5. *a)* All students: Draw the graph of $y = x^2$.

    b) Use the generalization you have agreed on to draw the following graphs:

    Student A: $y = x^2 - 2$
    Student B: $y = x^2 - 4.5$
    Student C: $y = x^2 + 5$

    Check one another's graphs.

(Continued)

Using Transformations to Graph Parabolas—Continued

Exercise 2

1. Draw the graphs of each of the following congruent parabolas:

$$\text{Student A: } y = (x - 1)^2$$
$$\text{Student B: } y = (x + 2)^2$$
$$\text{Student C: } y = (x - 3)^2$$

2. Superimpose the graph of $y = x^2$ on each of the three graphs in (1) so that, in each case, the *axes* coincide.

   In each case the group should state the transformation that can be used to obtain the new graph from the graph of $y = x^2$. Transformations:

   $y = (x - 1)^2$: _____

   $y = (x + 2)^2$: _____

   $y = (x - 3)^2$: _____

3. Find a generalization for a method of obtaining the graph of $y = (x - h)^2$ (*h* a real number) from the graph of $y = x^2$.

   Generalization: _____

4. Use the generalization you have agreed on to graph each of the following parabolas:

$$\text{Student A: } y = (x + 3)^2$$
$$\text{Student B: } y = (x - 4)^2$$
$$\text{Student C: } y = (x + 1)^2$$

Check one another's graphs.

Using Transformations to Graph Parabolas—Continued

Exercise 3

1. Decide within the group how one can best use the discoveries made in the two previous activities to draw the graph of $y = (x - 1)^2 + 3$ Draw the graph.

2. State a generalization for a method of obtaining the graph of $y = (x - h)^2 + k$ (h, k real numbers) from the graph of $y = x^2$.

   Generalization: _____

3. Draw the graph of $y = x^2 - 2x + 4$. Compare this graph with the graph of $y = (x - 1)^2 + 3$. What do you notice? Why is this so?

   _____

   _____

Exercise 4

1. Prepare a group summary of what you have learned from these activitles.

2. Suggest other similar explorations that might be made with the graphs of parabolas.

ACTIVITY 14: Review of Circles

Learning Level: Secondary school

Curriculum Area: Geometry

Objective:

To review the application of circle theorems

Group Size: Four or five students

Materials for Each Group:

   1 problem sheet for each student

Teaching Notes:

- The students are to complete the problem sheet as a homework assignment. The next day of class the students must agree on the solutions to the problems. A group gets credit for the correct solution only if any person who is called on in the group presents a correct explanation of the problem to the class.

- Similar problem sheets can be made to review work in other areas of the curriculum.

PROBLEM SHEET FOR ACTIVITY 14

Review of Circles

1. Complete the given exercises at home. State all theorems you used in each case.

2. Bring your completed assignment to class tomorrow for group discussion.

3. When the members of your group have agreed on the best solution for each problem, submit *one set* of solutions for your group.

4. Each person must be able to explain any of the group's solutions to the whole class.

Exercises

   a) In a circle whose radius is 10, a chord is 16 units long. Compute the distance of the chord from the center of the circle.

   b) Two concentric circles have radii of length 5 and 13 centimeters. Compute the length of a chord of the larger circle that is tangent to the smaller circle.

   c) From a point, *P*, outside circle *O*, a tangent $\overline{PC}$ is drawn. If the radius of the circle measures 8 centimeters and the tangent measures 15 centimeters, what is the distance, *PO*, from the point *P* to the center of the circle?

   d) In circle *O*, diameter $\overline{AB}$ measures 14 units. If chord $\overline{AC}$ measures 7 units, calculate the measure of angle *CAB*.

   e) The segment joining the midpoint of a chord to the midpoint of its minor arc has length 4 centimeters. If the chord itself has length 20 centimeters, find the length of the diameter of the circle.

   f) An equilateral pentagon is inscribed in a circle. Compute the measure of the angle formed by a side of the pentagon and a line tangent to the circle at one of the vertices of the pentagon.

ACTIVITY 15: Roots and Coefficients of Quadratic Equations

Learning Level: Secondary school

Curriculum Area: Algebra

Objectives:

1. To practice solving quadratic equations by factoring
2. To determine the relationship between the coefficients and the sum of the roots
3. To determine the relationship between the coefficients and the product of the roots

Group Size: Four students

Materials for Each Group:

 4 problem sheets

 1 record sheet

 3 problem envelopes:

 Envelope 1 contains four slips of paper, each with a different quadratic equation of the form $ax^2 + bx + c = 0$ $(a = 1)$.

 Envelope 2 contains four slips of paper, each with a different quadratic equation of the form $ax^2 + bx + c = 0$ $(a \neq 0$ and $a \neq 1)$.

 Envelope 3 contains four slips of paper, each with a quadratic equation of the form $ax^2 + bx + c = 0$ $(a \neq 0)$ different from those in envelopes 1 and 2.

Teaching Notes:

• In problem envelope 1, include four slips of paper. On each paper write a different equation (suggestions are listed below).

 1) $x^2 + 2x - 15 = 0$ 2) $x^2 + x - 6 = 0$

 3) $x^2 - 9x + 20 = 0$ 4) $x^2 - 4x - 12 = 0$

Since $a = 1$ in each of the equations above, the relationship is $r_1 + r_2 = -b$ and $r_1 \bullet r_2 = c$.

• In problem envelope 2, include four slips of paper. On each paper write a different equation (suggestions are listed below).

 1) $2x^2 + x - 3 = 0$ 2) $3x^2 + 11x - 4 = 0$

 3) $20x^2 + 19x + 3 = 0$ 4) $6x^2 - 19x + 10 = 0$

In these equations the students will notice that $r_1 + r_2 = -b/a$ and $r_1 \bullet r_2 = c/a$. They will then check to see that this relationship holds for the cases where $a = 1$.

PROBLEM SHEET FOR ACTIVITY 15

Roots and Coefficients of Quadratic Equations

Exercise 1

One person should read the instructions while other group members follow along. When the reader has completed the reading, others may question or explain the tasks and the requirements of the problem. When the group is ready to begin, each member should select, at random, one slip of paper from problem envelope 1.

1. Each person will receive a quadratic equation of the form $ax^2 + bx + c = 0$ ($a = 1$) that has roots r_1 and r_2. Analyze each equation to determine—

   a) the values of a, b, and c;

   b) the roots r_1 and r_2;

   c) the sum of the roots: $r_1 + r_2$;

   d) the product of the roots: $r_1 \cdot r_2$'

2. Each group member who has completed his or her part of the work should offer to help another member.

3. Students who have completed their work should exchange papers and check one another's results.

4. When all the equations have been analyzed and the group has agreed on the results, one student should list the results in the record sheet.

5. The group members should discuss their findings and determine—

   a) the relationship among the coefficients a, b, and c and the sum of the roots;

   _____

   b) the relationship among the coefficients a, b, and c and the product of the roots.

   _____

(Continued)

Roots and Coefficients of Quadratic Equations—Continued

Exercise 2

1. Each member of the group should select, at random, one slip of paper from problem envelope 2. Each person will receive a quadratic equation of the form $ax^2 + bx + c = 0$ ($a \neq 0$, $a \neq 1$), with the roots r_1 and r_2. Analyze each equation as in activity 1. (Find the values of a, b, c, r_1, r_2, $r_1 + r_2$, and $r_1 \cdot r_2$.)

2. When all the equations have been analyzed and the group has agreed on the results, one student should list the results on the record sheet.

3. The group members should discuss their findings and determine the relationships among the coefficients a, b, and c of the equation and the sum and product of the roots.

4. State the relationships.

   _____

   _____

5. Check to see that these relationships among the roots and coefficients apply to the previous equations having $a = 1$.

Exercise 3

1. Each member of the group should select, at random, one slip of paper from problem envelope 3. Each person will receive a quadratic equation of the form $ax^2 + bx + c = 0$. *Without solving the equation*, determine the sum and product of the roots. Write your answers on the paper.

2. Exchange papers. *Solve* the equation on the new slip of paper. Check to see that the sum and product of the roots, written on the slip of paper, agree with your solution.

3. If the results *do not agree,* the two students who determined the roots and the sum and product of the roots should discuss their findings and come to an agreement.

RECORD SHEET FOR ACTIVITY 15

Equation	r_1	r_2	a	b	c	$r_1 + r_2$	$r_1 \cdot r_1$

BIBLIOGRAPHY

Anderson, Mary. *Partnerships: Developing Teamwork at the Computer.* Santa Cruz, Calif.: Educational Apple-cations, 1988.

Andrini, Beth. *Cooperative Learning and Mathematics: A Multi-Structural Approach.* San Juan Capistrano, Calif.: Kagan Cooperative Learning, 1996.

Aronson, Elliot. *The Jigsaw Classroom.* Newbury Park, Calif.: Sage Publications, 1978.

Artzt, Alice F. *The Comparative Effects of the Student-Team Method of Instruction and the Traditional Teacher-Centered Method of Instruction upon Student Achievement, Attitude, and Social Interaction in High School Mathematics Courses.* Doctoral diss., New York University, 1983. University Microfilms (84-06277).

———. "Developing Problem-Solving Behaviors by Assessing Communication in Cooperative Learning Groups." In *Communication in Mathematics, K–12,* 1996 Yearbook of the National Council of Teachers of Mathematics, edited by Portia C. Elliott, pp. 116–25. Reston, Va.: National Council of Teachers of Mathematics, 1996.

———. "Integrating Writing and Cooperative Learning in the Mathematics Class." *Mathematics Teacher* 87 (February 1994): 80–85.

———. "Student Teams in Mathematics Class." *Mathematics Teacher* 72 (October 1979): 505–8.

Artzt, Alice F., and Eleanor Armour-Thomas. "Development of a Cognitive-Metacognitive Framework for Protocol Analysis of Mathematical Problem Solving in Small Groups." *Cognition and Instruction* 9 (1992): 137–75.

———. "Mathematical Problem Solving in Small Groups: Exploring the Interplay of Students' Metacognitive Behaviors, Perceptions, and Ability Levels." *Journal of Mathematical Behavior,* forthcoming.

Artzt, Alice F., and Claire M. Newman. "Cooperative Learning." *Mathematics Teacher* 83 (September 1990): 448–52.

Bassarear, Tom. "A Match Made in Heaven: NCTM Standards and Cooperative Learning." *Cooperative Learning* 14 (1994): 2–5.

Bassarear, Tom, and Neil Davidson. "The Use of Small Group Learning Situations in Mathematics Instruction as a Tool." In *Enhancing Thinking through Cooperative Learning,* edited by Neil Davidson and Toni Worsham, pp. 235–50. New York: Teachers College Press, 1992.

Behounek, Karla J., Linda J. Rosenbaum, Les Brown, and Janet V. Burcalow. "Our Class Has Twenty-five Teachers." *Arithmetic Teacher* 36 (December 1988): 10–13.

Cohen, Elizabeth G., and Joan Benton. "Making Groupwork Work." *American Educator* 12 (Fall 1988): 10–17, 45–46.

Curcio, Frances R., and Alice Artzt. "The Effects of Small Group Interaction on Graph Comprehension of Fifth Graders." Paper presented at the Seventh International Congress on Mathematical Education, Quebec City, Quebec, August 1992.

Davidson, Neil. "Small-Group Cooperative Learning in Mathematics: A Review of the Research." Unpublished manuscript.

———. "The Small-Group Discovery Method in Secondary- and College-Level Mathematics." In *Cooperative Learning in Mathematics: A Handbook for Teachers,* edited by Neil Davidson, pp. 335–61. Menlo Park, Calif.: Addison-Wesley, 1990a.

———. "Small-Group Learning and Teaching in Mathematics: A Selective Review of the Research." In *Learning to Cooperate, Cooperating to Learn,* edited by Robert Slavin, Shlomo Sharan, Spencer Kagan, Rachel Hertz-Lazarowitz, Clark Webb, and Richard Schmuck. New York: Plenum Publishing Corp., 1985.

———, ed. *Cooperative Learning in Mathematics: A Handbook for Teachers.* Menlo Park, Calif.: Addison-Wesley, 1990b.

Dees, Roberta L. "Cooperation in the Mathematics Classroom: A User's Manual." In *Cooperative Learning in Mathematics: A Handbook for Teachers,* edited by Neil Davidson, pp. 160–200. Menlo Park, Calif.: Addison-Wesley, 1990.

Dishon, Dee, and Pat O'Leary. *A Guidebook for Cooperative Learning: A Technique for Creating More Effective Schools.* Holmes Beach, Fla.: Learning Publications, 1984.

Dubois, Dion J. "Student Team Learning and Middle School Math." *Cooperative Learning* 14 (1994): 18–20.

Gilbert-Macmillan, Kathleen, and Steven Leitz. "Cooperative Small Groups: A Method for Teaching Problem Solving." *Arithmetic Teacher* 33 (March 1986): 9–11.

Graves, Nan, and Ted Graves. *Getting There Together: A Sourcebook and Desk-Top Guide for Creating a Cooperative Classroom.* Santa Cruz, Calif.: Cooperative College of California, 1988.

Johnson, David W., and Roger T. Johnson. *Cooperation and Competition: Theory and Research.* Edina, Minn.: Interaction Book Co., 1989.

———. "Cooperative Learning and Achievement." In *Cooperative Learning: Theory and Research,* edited by Shlomo Sharan. New York: Praeger Publishers, 1990.

———. "Cooperative Learning and Nonacademic Outcomes of Schooling." In *Secondary Schools and Cooperative Learning: Theories, Models, and Strategies,* edited by Jon E. Pedersen and Annette D. Bigby, pp. 81–152. New York: Garland Publishing, 1995.

———. "Critical Thinking through Structured Controversy." *Educational Leadership* 45 (1988): 58–64.

———. "Encouraging Thinking through Constructive Controversy." In *Enhancing Thinking through Cooperative Learning,* edited by Neil Davidson and Toni Worsham, pp. 120–37. New York: Teachers College Press, 1992a.

———. "Instructional Goal Structure: Cooperative, Competitive, or Individualistic." *Review of Educational Research* 44 (1974): 213–40.

———. *Learning Together and Alone.* Englewood Cliffs, N.J.: Prentice Hall, 1991.

———. *Learning Together and Alone: Cooperative, Competitive, and Individualistic Learning.* 2nd ed. Englewood Cliffs, N.J.: Prentice Hall, 1987.

———. "Positive Interdependence: Key to Effective Cooperation." In *Interaction in Cooperative Groups: The Theoretical Anatomy of Group Learning,* edited by Rachel Hertz-Lazarowitz and Norman Miller, pp. 174–99. New York: Cambridge University Press, 1992b.

———, eds. *Cooperative Learning: Warm-Ups, Grouping Strategies and Group Activities.* Edina, Minn.: Interaction Book Co., 1985.

Johnson, David W., Roger T. Johnson, and Edythe Johnson Holubec. *Revised Circles of Learning: Cooperation in the Classroom.* Edina, Minn.: Interaction Book Co., 1986.

Johnson, David W., Roger Johnson, and Geoffrey M. Maruyama. "Interdependence and Interpersonal Attraction among Heterogeneous and Homogeneous Individuals: A Theoretical Formulation and a Meta-Analysis of the Research." *Review of Educational Research* 52 (1983): 5–54.

Kagan, Spencer. *Cooperative Learning Resources for Teachers.* 4th ed. Laguna Niguel, Calif.: Resources for Teachers, 1987.

————. "Dimensions of Cooperative Classroom Structures." In *Learning to Cooperate, Cooperating to Learn,* edited by Robert Slavin, Shlomo Shaaran, Spencer Kagan, Rachel Hertz-Lazarowitz, Clark Webb, and Richard Schmuck. New York: Plenum Publishing Corp., 1985.

————. "The Structural Approach to Cooperative Learning." *Educational Leadership* 47 (December 1989/January 1990): 12–15.

Kroll, Diana Lambdin, Joanna O. Masingila, and Sue Tinsley Mau. "Grading Cooperative Problem Solving." *Mathematics Teacher* 85 (November 1992): 619–27.

Lambdin, Diana K. "Monitoring Moves and Roles in Cooperative Mathematical Problem Solving." *Focus on Learning Problems in Mathematics* 15 (Spring and Summer 1993): 48–64.

Ma, Xin, and Nand Kishor. "Assessing the Relationship between Attitude toward Mathematics and Achievement in Mathematics: A Meta-Analysis." *Journal for Research in Mathematics Education* 28 (January 1997): 26–47.

Male, Mary. "Cooperative Learning and Computers in the Elementary and Middle School Math Classroom." In *Cooperative Learning in Mathematics: A Handbook for Teachers,* edited by Neil Davidson, pp. 126–59. Menlo Park, Calif.: Addison-Wesley, 1990.

Male, Mary, David Johnson, Roger Johnson, and Mary Anderson. *Cooperative Learning and Computers.* Santa Cruz, Calif.: Educational Apple-cations, 1987.

McDonald, Penny. *Cooperation at the Computer: A Handbook for Using Software with Cooperative Learning Groups.* Palatine, Ill.: Skylight Publishing Co., 1989.

National Council of Supervisors of Mathematics. "Essential Mathematics for the Twenty-first Century: The Position of the National Council of Supervisors of Mathematics." *Mathematics Teacher* 82 (May 1989): 388–91.

National Council of Teachers of Mathematics. *Assessment Standards for School Mathematics.* Reston, Va.: National Council of Teachers of Mathematics, 1995.

————. *Curriculum and Evaluation Standards for School Mathematics.* Reston, Va.: National Council of Teachers of Mathematics, 1989.

————. *Professional Standards for Teaching Mathematics.* Reston, Va.: National Council of Teachers of Mathematics, 1991.

National Research Council. *Everybody Counts: A Report to the Nation on the Future of Mathematics Education.* Washington, D.C.: National Academy Press, 1989.

Noddings, Nel. "Constructivism in Mathematics Education." In *Constructivist Views of the Teaching and Learning of Mathematics,* edited by Robert B. Davis, Carolyn Maher, and Nel Noddings, pp. 7–18. Reston, Va.: National Council of Teachers of Mathematics, 1990.

Owens, John E. "Cooperative Learning in Secondary Mathematics: Research and Theory." In *Secondary Schools and Cooperative Learning: Theories, Models, and Strategies,* edited by Jon E. Pedersen and Annette D. Digby, pp. 281–301. New York: Garland Publishing, 1995.

Qin, Zhining, David W. Johnson, and Roger T. Johnson. "Cooperative versus Competitive Efforts and Problem Solving." *Review of Educational Research* 65 (Summer 1995): 129–43.

Robertson, Laurel, Neil Davidson, and Roberta Dees. "The Teacher's Role in Cooperative Mathematics Lessons." *Cooperative Learning* 14 (1994): 8–12.

Rosenbaum, Linda, Karla J. Behounek, Les Brown, and Janet V. Burcalow. "Step into Problem Solving with Cooperative Learning." *Arithmetic Teacher* 36 (March 1989): 7–11.

Sharan, Shlomo. "Cooperative Learning in Small Groups: Recent Methods and Effects on Achievement, Attitudes and Ethnic Relations." *Review of Educational Research* 50 (1980): 241–71.

Sharan, Shlomo, and Rachel Hertz-Lazarowitz. "A Group Investigation Method of Cooperative Learning in the Classroom." In *Cooperation in Education,* edited by Shlomo Sharan, P. Hare, Clark Webb, and Rachel Hertz-Lazarowitz, pp. 14–46. Provo, Utah: Brigham Young University Press, 1980.

Sharan, Yael, ed. *Cooperative Learning: Theory and Research.* New York: Praeger Publishers, 1990.

Sharan, Yael, and Shlomo Sharan. *Expanding Cooperative Learning through Group Investigation.* New York: Teachers College Press, 1992.

——. "Group Investigation Expands Cooperative Learning." *Educational Leadership* 47 (December 1989/January 1990): 17–21.

Sheets, Charlene, and M. Kathleen Heid. "Integrating Computers as Tools in Mathematics Curricula (Grades 9–13): Portraits of Group Interactions." In *Cooperative Learning in Mathematics: A Handbook for Teachers,* edited by Neil Davidson, pp. 265–94. Menlo Park, Calif.: Addison-Wesley, 1990.

Slavin, Robert E. "Cooperative Learning." *Review of Educational Research* 50 (1980a): 315–42.

——. *Cooperative Learning.* New York: Longman, 1983.

——. "Cooperative Learning and Achievement: An Empirically-Based Theory." Paper presented at the annual meeting of the American Educational Research Association, Atlanta, April 1993.

——. "Cooperative Learning and Individualized Instruction." *Arithmetic Teacher* 35 (November 1987): 7–13.

——. "Cooperative Learning and Student Achievement." *Educational Leadership* 46 (October 1988): 31–33.

——. *Cooperative Learning: Theory, Research, and Practice.* Englewood Cliffs, N.J.: Prentice Hall, 1990.

———. "Research on Cooperative Learning: Consensus and Controversy." *Educational Leadership* 47 (December 1989/January 1990): 52–54.

———. *School and Classroom Organization.* Hillsdale, N.J.: Lawrence Erlbaum Associates, 1989.

———. *Using Student Team Learning.* Rev. ed. Baltimore: Center for Social Organization of Schools, Johns Hopkins University, 1980b.

———. "When Does Cooperative Learning Increase Student Achievement?" *Psychological Bulletin* 94 (1983): 429–45.

Slavin, Robert E., Marshall Leavey, and Nancy Madden. "Combining Cooperative Learning and Individualized Instruction: Effects on Student Mathematics Achievement, Attitudes, and Behaviors." *Elementary School Journal* 84 (1984): 7–13.

Slavin, Robert E., Nancy Madden, and Marshall Leavey. "Effects of Team Assisted Individualization on the Mathematics Achievement of Academically Handicapped and Nonhandicapped Students." *Journal of Educational Psychology* 76 (1984): 813–19.

Slavin, Robert E., Shlomo Sharan, Spencer Kagan, Rachel Hertz-Lazarowitz, Clark Webb, and Richard Schmuck. *Learning to Cooperate, Cooperating to Learn.* New York: Plenum Publishing Corp., 1985.

Smith, Tommy, Susan Williams, and Norma Wynn. "Cooperative Group Learning in the Secondary Mathematics Classroom." In *Secondary Schools and Cooperative Learning: Theories, Models, and Strategies,* edited by Jon E. Pedersen and Annette D. Digby, pp. 281–301. New York: Garland Publishing, 1995.

Sutton, Gail O. "Cooperative Learning Works in Mathematics." *Mathematics Teacher* 85 (January 1992): 63–66.

Suydam, Marilyn. "Research Report: Individualized or Cooperative Learning." *Arithmetic Teacher* 32 (April 1985): 39.

Vygotsky, Lev S. *Mind in Society: The Development of Higher Psychological Processes.* Cambridge, Mass.: Harvard University Press, 1978.

Webb, Noreen M. "Peer Interaction and Learning in Small Groups." *International Journal of Educational Research* 13 (1989): 21–39.

———. "Student Interaction and Learning in Small Groups: A Research Summary." In *Learning to Cooperate, Cooperating to Learn,* edited by Robert Slavin, Shlomo Sharan, Spencer Kagan, Rachel Hertz-Lazarowitz, Clark Webb, and Richard Schmuck. New York: Plenum Publishing Corp., 1985.

———. "Student Interaction and Mathematics Learning in Small Groups." Unpublished manuscript.

———. "Task-Related Verbal Interaction and Mathematics Learning in Small Groups." *Journal for Research in Mathematics Education* 22 (November 1991): 366–89.